27/6/1

When Will I See You Again?

Experiences of migration and separation in
childhood - from the Caribbean to Britain

Edited by
Zindika Kamauesi
Natalie Smith

Pen Press Publishers Ltd

First published in Great Britain by
Pen Press Publishers Ltd
39-41 North Road
London N7 9DP

Printed and bound in the UK

ISBN 1-904018-27-0

A catalogue record of this book is available
from the British Library

Cover design by Bridget Tyldsley

This book is dedicated to L.A.McIntyre (Papa) and those grandmothers who cared for many the best way they could.

Identity means to discover oneself.
It must be that the greatest injustice to any man is the destruction
of his identity.

Juanita Apenya

Today, each man must work at telling his own story if he is to be
able to reclaim his personal identity.

Sheldon Kopp

CONTENTS

'History is a clock that people use to tell the political and cultural time of day. It is also a compass that people use to find themselves on the map of human geography. History tells a people where they have been and what they have been, what they are and, most important, history tells a people where they still must go and what they still must be. The relationship of history to the people is the same as the relationship of a mother to her child.'

John Henrik Clarke - *A Great and Mighty Walk*

FOREWORD

It is always difficult when time has passed, to accurately identify the forces which have motivated an action, to unwind the skein of the threads of growth, and to trace those threads back through the complexities of later developments. It was with those thoughts in mind that I undertook to introduce this book to you. When I was asked to write this Foreword, I read some of the stories and my thoughts went immediately to two of my black women colleagues in the House of Lords: Baroness Valerie Amos and Baroness Patricia Scotland. Both Valerie and Patricia are high-achieving career women and now prominent members of the House. They both came over from the Caribbean to join their parents when they were children. They are both successful examples of the experiences this book addresses.

This is a book based on the real life experiences of a group of young people who share a journey, unique to themselves, and in the telling have uncovered how much their experiences have a certain commonality - being left behind, then being reunited.

Coming from similar backgrounds unites them; learning to adjust to new families, a new country with a totally different culture and not a little hostility, is well captured within the following pages. The writers have retraced their journeys in a pure and honest way. Reading this book will take the reader through some painful, sometimes funny and attention holding reminiscences which only the authors themselves could relate.

Their application varies - but that in itself is important to the work as the writers are a unique group of survivors in the struggle for acceptance in an environment which has many faces. I have been educated reading this work.

As we struggle in Britain with diversity, their narrative provides some answers for 21st century Britain.

I hope everyone will read this book.

Ros Howells
Baroness Howells of St. Davids, OBE

INTRODUCTION

*The black mother in not being able to mother
her children is unprecedented in the amount of time
spent apart from her offspring - whether it be
because of slavery, domestic work, or migration -
separation (whether by forces of circumstance or free
will) has become an integral part of the black mother
and child relationship.*

Many years ago in the sixties our parents left Jamaica in the
mass exodus to England to seek a better future. They left
behind four children - the youngest a baby and the oldest about
aged six. They took with them one child and later had another
child born in England. In our family migration meant separation
- from parents, the splitting up of siblings, separation from
grandparents and the extended family, separation from a
community and a country. Our family has never been fully
reunited. The years away from our parents was never spoken
about or fully acknowledged. We had lived a life without them
and this life had locked us all into a separate existence. In the
Caribbean we had grown up with strangers who had become
our family, whilst in Britain our family had become like strangers.

Ours is by no means a unique experience. Many children
experienced separation as a result of migration from the
Caribbean to Britain during the '50s-'70s - a period which is
the focus of this book.

Migration is about betterment. The courage of the first

generation who came over to start afresh is highly regarded and vastly recognised; less is known about those who made the first voyage as children. Many children were left behind in the Caribbean whilst their parents went abroad in search of better opportunities and to seek a new life for themselves and their families. In some sense the Caribbean childhood was quite idyllic, but these children felt a sense of abandonment as what was to be a brief sojourn for their parents became permanent. Some were left as babies and toddlers with the promise that they would be sent for soon and did not see their parents again until they were virtual adults. During this time, the air fares went up, immigration laws changed, some parents remained indecisive as to whether they were staying or returning and kept their children on tenterhooks. Some children never saw their parents again; as they settled, started new families and forgot about the old ones back home thereby severing all ties permanently.

Their stories are part of a 'secret history'. Secret in the sense that it is hardly ever talked about, often brushed over or dismissed. As immigrant children, we (the editors) have often questioned the legacy of separation that has shaped our own lives and that of our family. We have questioned and debated the psychological effect of separation and displacement on the parents and children involved in the upheaval. The reasons for the movement is immeasurably clear. Parents were forced out by poverty, unemployment and the pursuit of a decent education for their children, but the damage caused by separation has left deep rifts in some families and painful scars for many of the children. Often they were left without explanation and without adequate financial support. Later they were received in England still without explanation and often with little affection. Some parents did not have the time or inclination to catch up with the missing years in their children's life. Mostly they were too busy working, or bringing up a new family which they had started in England. Some of these children who came over were abused, ill-treated, ignored and became like strangers in their own families. No one seemed concerned that these children may have suffered multiple separations in their early lives from family, and that coming to England later meant further separation from grandparents and the wider extended family.

BACKGROUND

The history of Black people in the west is one of dispersal, first through slavery and then migration. This pattern of dispersal is perpetuated by the contemporary black family plagued by issues of single motherhood and absentee fathers. The separation of the African mother and child is nothing new. The present family structure as we see it in the Caribbean is very much the by-product of slavery which separated men from women and women from children.

Stage One: Starts with the capturing of slaves in West Africa. Slaves were not captured in family groupings but as individuals - which inevitably meant that leaving Africa for the new world, they were leaving behind, mothers, fathers and children.

Stage Two: Once on the plantations - slaves belonged to their white masters and were property to be bought and sold. Their children were also property to be bought and sold and often were. Therefore there was little maintenance of family life.

Stage Three: The abolishment of slavery in 1838 in the Caribbean left a fragmented pattern of family life. Union amongst the men and women of the poorer class took the form of 'common law' and 'non legal concubinage'. This pattern of liaison and cohabiting freed the men of responsibility for individual households leaving women in charge. Therefore households became matriarchal although not necessarily mother focused - but very much dependent on a large extended family of grandmothers, aunties and older female siblings who took responsibility for children and their upbringing.

Stage Four: Migration saw the continuation of the scattering of the African diaspora families. Many people migrated to the USA, Canada, England and elsewhere. Usually the men went first and was followed by their wives and children, or wives and then children, causing further disruptions to family life.

Stage Five: The African-Caribbean family now severed from its African roots must adapt to the western concept of the nuclear family - but it is further thwarted by high unemployment, economic poverty and racial oppression. All the above have virtually obliterated the African-Caribbean family both in the traditional and modern sense.

Although this book does not nurture any idealistic notions of the 2.2 nuclear family structure which is hardly a reality today, it does recognise that any semblance of the black family that remains is as a result of the stamina of black women. Without negating the experiences of black men who participate - the central relationships of most families tend to revolve around the mother. Women head households in significant numbers of Caribbean homes; women tend to be affected more by upheavals in the family; therefore it is not surprising that many of our contributors focused on the loss of the mother/child bond and how it affected their lives.

In the social and historical movement of black people, black women's role as mothers, workers and political campaigners have always been at the forefront of change. Whereas white women have always viewed work as a liberating experience from patriarchy, for black women faced with racial and economic oppression, work became a means of survival. However, the demanding and exploitative nature of the work available left them tired, without the energy or time for nurturing and caring for their own families.

'. . . we can see that internationally; the black mammy figure has become a personification of all the housework, the labour that black women had to do in those days of slavery and continue to do after the abolition of slavery...

What did the work of the mammy (black women) involve? It involved reproducing everyone, and by that I mean not just bearing children, but raising them, looking after them, other women, yourself, making sure that everyone was fit for the next day. And reproducing not only her own children, her man and herself, but also reproducing the master and his family, his children, his wife and for satisfying the master sexually. The mammy was responsible for keeping everyone going.'

- Margaret Prescod:
Black Women: Bringing it all back home

Sit in any park on a sunny day in certain New York neighbourhoods, and you will observe an every day sight of the park filling up with adults and children. Nothing is unusual about this except for one thing, virtually all the children will be white and all the adults black women - otherwise known as domestic workers, or nannies. Most of these women are Caribbean and a few Hispanics.

The interaction between these women and children is interesting. The children want affection from the women, but the women are uncomfortable with this, or unsure of how to give this affection in public. Most of these women probably have their own children whom they have left behind in the Caribbean, being cared for by grandparents, and the white children whom they care for, clearly want their parents. This, and similar scenarios repeat themselves in other parts of the world. (Documented in 'SILENCED' Caribbean Domestic Workers - the Canadian experience by Makeda Silvera). Black women abandoning their children for economic survival and the black family being torn apart. The never-ending struggle of the black woman who is called on to mother the world while her own children are starved of affection and her physical presence is nothing new. Some things never go away.

> *Our great-great-grandmothers were wounded.*
> *They were slaves, property, chattel; denied the basic*
> *right to think for themselves.*
> *They were mentally, emotionally, and spiritually*
> *wounded. They passed their wounded images and*
> *ideas on to our great-grandmothers, who passed*
> *them onto our mothers, who passed them onto us. We*
> *are today the walking wounded of our foremothers.*
>
>   Iyanla Vanzant, 'The Value in the Valley'

Homeopathy is a branch of alternative medicine in which you cure like with like. It is regarded that if an illness took ten years to develop it will likely to take ten years to cure. Healing is a part of that process. A wounded soldier hampers the troops. Black women are spearheading the healing revolution in the '90s and we are going from strength to strength.

> *Read fictional narrative where black women*
> *break through the silences to speak the truth of their*
> *lives. To give testimony has helped individual black*
> *women take the risk to openly share painful*
> *experiences. Collective healing can only take*

place when we face reality. . . there is no healing in
silence.

bell hooks, 'Sisters of the Yam'

The stages outlined have been long and laborious, but like precious metal we shall emerge from this compression golden and pristine like. Our true value and purpose is yet to behold.

THE BOOK

The book is an anthology. It is both historical and contemporary and is aimed at a broad cross-section of people. It incorporates a mixture of styles in the form of poetry, short stories, letters and interviews

It was important to get a wide range of contributors from different islands and a balance of men and women. Inevitably the women outnumbered the men and so it does become a woman focused book but we have tried to compensate by our interviews with men.

The book has four sections:

HOME AND AWAY: Which looks at the idyllic Caribbean childhood and memories of halcyon days. It is an attempt to pay tribute to those grandmothers who took up the mantle of care and to capture the pain of leaving and the joy of arrival.

LANDING AND REUNION: An honest attempt to explore feelings and the impact of separation - how it affected family relationships and the difficulties of adjusting not just to a new environment but to families that were relative strangers.

PUTTING DOWN ROOTS: Adjusting to a new environment and the fact that England was now home.

THE MEANING OF THE JOURNEY: Those who

came over as children are now the adults of today, they are parents, with children and careers. What have they made of the opportunities that England offered and how do they view the future?

Although we have tried to keep clear sections, inevitably there must be some overlapping. Most people wanted to write about their experience of being there and coming here, and the impact of adjusting to a new country was a major theme that cropped up in most of the pieces. Not everyone who responded to our adverts for contributors ended up writing. For some people the experience was too painful, others did not view themselves as writers as the book required a creative edge rather than being academically researched. However, we hope that this book reflects and represent their experience. This book is a rare chance to air, share and celebrate the experiences of a quiet minority.

Although this is a book which looks back, it is also a book that looks forward. There are new immigrants coming into the country - they will be leaving their children behind or bringing them here. We hope that this book will have a positive and encouraging effect on their lives and aspirations.

                                        Zindika Kamauesi
                                        Natalie Smith
                                        2002

HISTORICAL OVERVIEW

Today in Britain, the Caribbean population stands at just over half a million people - a far cry from the 500, mainly ex-servicemen who docked at Tilbury in Kent in 1948 and heralded the first significant civilian entry of Caribbeans to British shores.

Although there were several thousand Caribbean born peoples already living in Britain, the arrival of these men on board the Empire Windrush is nationally recognised as the event that spiralled the movement of Caribbeans to Britain.

Over fifty years on, and now into a fourth generation, Caribbeans however, constitute less than 1.5 percent of the population, half of them British born and the majority being from Jamaica or their descendants.

It was Jamaicans who largely answered the early call to fill a vacuum in the labour force, brought about as a result of the Second World War. Barbadians, Guyanese and Trinidadians were the next biggest groups to 'volunteer' their labour to help the 'Mother Country' in difficult times.

History has well documented the nature of the work Caribbeans were invited to do. On the whole, anti-social, industrial and service industry type jobs were readily available to these arrivees. While the indigenous population moved upwards and considered such jobs beneath them, large public and government bodies embraced immigrants from the Caribbean to meet the labour shortfall.

British agencies even took the steps of going to the Caribbean in their recruitment drive to entice people to take up jobs here. With many islands in poor economic conditions, people were keen to respond. In the '50s for example, Barbados became prime ground for British Transport, hotels, restaurants and hospital boards who sent teams there directly to recruit sponsored labour in conjunction with the Barbadian government.

With these early patterns, the precedent was set for the type of jobs likely to be open to Caribbean people in the future, and today there still remain a sizeable proportion of Caribbeans employed in these areas.

The 1991 census showed that of Caribbeans of working age (16+), over 75 percent participate in the labour force, with over two thirds skewed towards manual labour, compared to about half the white population. And of all the minority ethnic groups in Britain, black Caribbeans have the least number of people working in the 'professional' fields. Other communities, such as Asians and Jews, have noticeably moved upwards with clearly identifiable middle class segments, whilst Caribbeans have on the whole remained in the lower economic class, with few owning homes, businesses or moving out of inner city areas.

Thus, coming to the 'Mother country' for Caribbeans did not fulfil the dreams many had hoped for themselves, their children, and ensuing generations.

There are now some 300,000 British born Caribbeans in Britain. This figure will continue to rise as the older generation die off or return home. Although there are new economic immigrants arriving, from Jamaica in particular, the number of Caribbean born peoples here is unlikely to reach the heights of the early '60s when Caribbeans arrived here in their thousands.

Since the early '70s immigration from the Caribbean could be said to be effectively over. Most of those who have arrived since have been the spouses and children of those who settled here earlier.

As new immigrants were arriving to join relatives, the government was simultaneously seeking to bring in legislation to cut down on the number of black people coming into the country. Although tiny by comparison to white immigration, such as the Irish, black immigrants were viewed as not fitting in with the character of the British landscape, and the 'Commonwealth Immigration Act' of 1962 was one of several pieces of legislation brought in to try and curb the numbers of 'coloured' people coming to Britain.

Enoch Powell is probably the most noted politician of his day to voice directly what many politicians on all sides of the house were saying in more covert ways. His landmark 'Rivers Of Blood' speech in 1968 happened in the same year as the Labour Government introduced the second Commonwealth Immigration Act which sought to control mainly East African Asian immigration.

The racial basis to the act was clear, and Powell's tirade that racial tension would be increased along the lines of what was happening in America, popularised the racist message amongst the masses. Images of whites being unable to get hospital beds, children unable to get school places, or neighbourhoods being overrun with 'coloured' faces were left imprinted on the consciousness of white British people, who largely believed him.

Although a race war did not materialise as predicted by Powell, it did not stop Margaret Thatcher trying to stir up racial tension in the '80s, by referring to people of 'an alien culture' swamping Britain.

The obvious difference in skin colouring made it easy, for governments and the white population to focus their attention on black people. Despite white immigrant groups outnumbering blacks; with poor jobs and living in slum conditions, black people were nevertheless accused of stealing jobs (that no one wanted) and depriving the indigenous people of their homes.

Caribbeans who did try to work their way out of their poverty-ridden lifestyle were usually met with resistance from individuals and businesses alike. Mortgages, for example, were virtually impossible to gain from banks, so only the determined or better-off could afford to purchase their home. With whites generally refusing to rent rooms to black families, early Caribbean settlers had to rely on the few black landlords to accommodate them in houses that also housed several other families.

These homes were cramped and dangerous, but with no other choice, families were forced to remain in these stressful conditions. Children who came to join families were brought into these environments, which caused added problems for them at school as they were not in environments that were conducive to them being able to study or settle long term.

A National Housing Survey carried out in the '70s showed that overcrowding for Caribbeans was four times that of whites, and three times as many Caribbeans as whites shared communal facilities such as a bathroom.

Although conditions have changed drastically since, today over 80 percent of Caribbeans still live in large cities such as London, Birmingham and Manchester. London is where most of the early immigrants came, and have remained, with over 50 percent of Caribbeans still residing there. London is also where many of the early attacks on black people by whites took place. The believed politicians like Powell that people of an alien background were swamping their country.

Attacks, both physical and verbal, have continued on black people throughout their time here. The case of murdered black teenager Stephen Lawrence has highlighted the distance there is still to go in terms of race relations in Britain. However, with large groups of Eastern Europeans and Africans being the new face of immigration to Britain, Caribbeans are now one of the older immigrant groups. The 1991 census showed there to be 22,000 Barbadian, 142,000 Jamaican, 17,000 Trinidadian and 60,000 from other Caribbean islands born here.

Now into a fourth generation, the second generation of the '60s and '70s, many of whom came here as children are the parents and grandparents today. Some of their stories are told in this book.

Home and Away

When the call went out in the '50s and the '60s from Britain to the Caribbean for workers to fill the void in the British labour force, many thousands answered. They sold what they could to afford the passage, and left in a hurry. Unsure of their destiny but expecting great things they probably did not have enough time to think about any consequences, or plan a proper farewell to those they were leaving behind.

As the years grew numerous, children who did not make the initial journey waited for the call from their parents. Some did not receive this invitation, but the 'lucky' ones were eventually re-united with their families. Leaving thus took on a whole new meaning; particularly for those who had grown old enough to almost forget they had parents abroad. Feelings were mixed. Excitement filled with fear; looking forward but always knowing they would be looking back to those that could not accompany them.

Grandparents were usually the people left behind with tears in their eyes and an empty heart, as those they had loved and cared for were taken away from them for a 'better life', one that they could not deny them.

For the young people who had heard so much about England and the good life, they could not wait to experience it for themselves. Parents had often failed to impress upon them the realities of life here, and apart from knowing it was cold, knew precious else that was real. When confirmation came that they were indeed, finally going to England, though elated they were unsure whether to laugh or cry. Any happiness would always be tinged with sadness of being parted from familiar people, surroundings and loved ones.

In Vernella Fuller's story, Elizabeth is stunned and upset when she overhears her grandmother referring to her being 'sent for' to go to England, and she cannot understand why her sister seems unconcerned about them 'Leaving Aunt Bea' to join their parents. Some recalled saying goodbye to grandparents as the most difficult moment in their life.

For the majority of children it would be the first time going anywhere. Coming from small islands they were not accustomed to travelling far from home. Yet there they were, about to take on a mammoth first journey. Friends and neighbours 'envied' them and made them promise to return to see them, and they swore to grandparents never to forget them. In their young minds everything seemed possible as vows were made to ensure that their grandparents were financially secure into their last years. People stocked them up with home produce to bring to relatives, knowing it would be their last taste of home for sometime and asked them to send a little piece of England. They said 'yes' and meant it.

To picture the scene, on a smaller scale try to remember the time you left home to face the adult world. Or, if a parent, recall what it was like when your first child decided to pack their bags and leave home. Though they may have moved only a few miles you felt abandoned but knew you could not deny them their future. However, they were within easy reach, at the other end of the phone line, and so you were reassured. Migrant children then, hoped but did not know if they would see their grandparents again.

Friends also had to be bid farewell, new clothes and shoes bought and appearances groomed, ready for

England. Yvonne James, tells us of how she was made presentable by her 'Tantie' for her journey to England. "First she had to sort out my hair...she had to put it right...My hair was straightened with a hot iron comb, curled with hot curling tongs...stinging burn marks on the earlobes and the nape of my neck were a constant reminder that I had to look perfect for Mummy and Daddy."

For many children, things that were not an issue before, such as their appearance, came sharply into focus. They were after all, going to the motherland and had to be impossibly perfect. The day finally came and they boarded their flights. Hours later they stepped off...their new lives had begun.

YVONNE JAMES

I was born on the beautiful island of St. Vincent in the Caribbean and spent a magical early childhood there. I came to join my parents in England in 1964 and have remained in this country ever since.

I live in Buckinghamshire with my family, pet chinchillas and fish. I am a teacher in a large secondary school. I love amateur dramatics and music. I am interested in environmental issues. I have always been concerned about the spraying of crops and the long term effects on the ecosystem of St. Vincent. I am also concerned about the plight and rights of the disabled.

I like to write about my early childhood and to rediscover and appreciate the language of my early days. I also like to perform my poetry.

Next Year Finally Comes

I awoke with an overwhelming feeling of excitement and panic. This was the day we had been waiting for, the beginning of our long journey across the skies from our beautiful island home of St. Vincent to England. At last after five years my six year old brother and I were to be reunited with our mum and dad.

It was before dawn, pitch black, deadly quiet, the cock had not even crowed yet. Tantie Carmen, or Tantie Mammy, as my brother affectionately called her, woke us early because we had to get the one and only bus to Kingstown. There was no time for a quick, refreshing, early morning bath - just time to get dressed and run. We were to stay with Tantie Emerline for three days before we travelled to England. It was her duty to ensure that we were presentable to our mum and dad.

Tantie Carmen had packed our suitcases over a period of days. Our suitcases were filled with goodies from our friends and neighbours, who had kissed, hugged, and wished us good luck and a bright and happy future. It would be strange not to see Miss Moor again. She was a mysterious old lady who filled me with fear and respect. She was our local herbalist, and had a special gift of healing. She always looked out for us and we were mindful of our behaviour when she was around. She even had a spy, a black and white dog called Teddy, who I'm sure carried news to her. She gave us cinnamon, mauby bark, spiced cocoa sticks and trumpets bush in case we got colds. We also had ferrine, sorrel blooms, half ripe mangoes and Zabuca (avocado pears), green, pungent smelling alcolado, limocal (all supposedly very good for colds), a small selections of yams and favourite fruits. Tantie even sent some strong rum for Daddy. Our neighbours also sent tokens to their relatives and I promised to write to my best friend Glorianna Peters and we promised to be best friends forever.

Ours was a farming community, villagers tilled the fertile volcanic slopes and took the fruits of their labours to market early in the morning. We made our way in the half light through our tiny hamlets of Bequia to Dickson Village where people congregated with their provisions for market. People boarded the bus with their sack and baskets of yams, tanya, cassava, mangoes, plums, coconuts, bananas, tomatoes and spices. Soon the big wooden bus had set off along the winding coast road to Kingstown, past the sleeping village store, the parlour where we bought refreshing mauby and penny bread. I looked down at my great grandmother's house and remembered her love. No more Sunday worship in the Save Soul church I thought. We left the familiar village and journeyed into the unknown.

Tantie Emerline, who was really our great aunt was to now take care of us after we had said a tearful goodbye to Tantie Mammy, who promised to come to see us in England 'next year'. She welcomed us with a kiss then set about making us presentable for Mum and Dad. First she had to sort out my hair. Part of it was red because it was burnt by the sun, or was it due to lack of certain vitamins, anyway, she had to put it right. My hair was straightened with a hot iron comb, curled with hot curling tongs and greased and blackened with the black crayon-type stick. The heat from the comb sent shivers down my spine, fear made it impossible for me to keep still. Stinging burn marks on the earlobes and the nape of my neck were a constant reminder that I had to look perfect for Mummy and Daddy. I'm sure that they would have loved us as we were. I didn't know that there was anything wrong with my hair. I became conscious and a little ashamed of the reddish brown streaks for sometime.

The wonderful day had arrived, to begin our journey to England. We were given various messages and promised faithfully to pass them on. We were to travel with a young woman who we had never seen before, but we weren't bothered because we were filled with wonder, awe and happiness. We became like seasoned travellers, flying on a tiny hopper to Barbados where we spent the night because of engine trouble. I don't remember how or where we slept, but I remembered that there was hot mud bubbling springs jumping in the air - it seemed so unreal.

The journey took us to Barbados, Trinidad, New York and finally on to England.

We were lucky, that Tantie Carmen had treated us as her own. Life on the island was fun, especially down by little river. Sunlight streamed through coconut branches and danced off the surface of the cool, clear water. Silvery grey trumpet bush overhung the river bank, watercress and dasheen leaves lined the margins. We caught crayfish in wicker baskets, lobsters in bamboo traps and prized black suckstone fish from black volcanic rocks. Occasionally a light aeroplane hovered overhead, spraying a crop of banana and people. Crayfish tasted sweet in Tantie's callaloo soup with coconut milk, slimy eddoes and cornmeal dumpling made my mouth water.

It was a mysterious place to me. I remember a stranger in rolled up khaki trousers stood barebacked by a large plantain tree. His hair was worn long in matted plaits, a style I had never seen before. I called out to everyone "Look at that man by the plantain tree." Nobody saw him.

Little River was a place for play and work. Tantie washed our clothes with a big bar of yellow soap and even blue Tide and Surf powder. I almost mastered the high pitched music as clothes and suds and water played through fingers. Will I need the skill of beating clothes on rock just so and putting them out to bleach in the sun in England? Did people beat clothes in

England? They say that people paper their walls with money in England, money even grows on trees, everyone is rich, that's what they say. But I knew I would miss the houses on the hill with the red galvanised iron roof and wooden tiles, the big mahogany four poster bed, my favourite hiding place, especially when the strange men came in their frightening silver-white suits, spraying crops with unknown chemicals.

Our happiest moments came when we received a registered letter from Mummy and Daddy, and better still, when Tantie walked home from the post office balancing a precious parcel on her head. It felt good. Everybody could see that Mummy and Daddy remembered us.

Even though Tantie treated us like her own, we had to work. I used to like to help carry water from the standpipe, a meeting place to exchange secrets with Glorianna and Sylvia. We laughed and splashed each other with water. We helped Tantie sweep the yard, wash the wares and feed the goats. Sometimes I fanned the flames to keep the fire going in the coalpot. Tantie didn't know that my cousin Jane changed her plaits when she was out of sight on the way to school, they looked like horns sticking out of her head and she didn't like that style. Sometimes I followed Jane to school. We were like sisters. I got vexed when she nearly ate off all the saltfish by the time we got home, and Tantie gave her a good slap she never forgot.

I remember a dream I had where I walked along the winding forest path flanked by spice trees, nutmeg, cinnamon and cloves; blossom did fall and kiss my face. The rainbow coloured spray was gone from the parched silent waterfall. Bullfrog didn't catch mongoose and agouti were long gone, not even lizard was basking in the sun. I was completely alone in a world of silence. There was an old wooden hut in the distance and as I got closer and closer, the tired door slowly opened. I awoke screaming with terror, Tantie was a comfort to me.

As we flew through the clouds, with thoughts of Tantie and

the home I was leaving I felt lighter than air and free, but trapped. As I looked down everything looked like a map, a drawing, not real. I almost pinched myself to see if I was dreaming. We were overjoyed when the pilot announced that we were about to land. "Fasten your seatbelts." I felt sick as my insides seemed to be sucked down to my toes.

I held my little brother's hand tightly as we climbed down the steps of the aeroplanes. I was excited and scared. I was wearing a red pleated woollen skirt, a white blouse, a yellow cardigan with a red and black pattern and a pair of black patent shoes with silver buckles. I smoothed down my clothes and brushed back my hair. I wanted to look my best for my parents, I wanted them to be proud of us. My brother wore a pair of grey trousers, a white shirt, and a red pullover, a grey jacket and black lace-up shoes with grey socks. We were in the care of a young woman who was going to stay with her aunt. She kept us under her wing. I don't even remember her name, but she helped to make a possibly terrifying experience more bearable.

I looked at all the faces of the strange people as we got off the plane. We shivered on that freezing February morning in 1964. Teeth chattered as I looked around for Mum and Dad. Would they be as I imagined them? I hoped that they would love us. How would I know them when I saw them? Would they know us? Would my little brother, who we had never seen, like us? I was frightened. This was the beginning of our life together. We had waited for so many years to be reunited with our parents.

When our friends back home asked, 'When you going to England to meet your Mammy and Daddy?' We would always say, 'Next year.' It was next year as far back as I could remember. Now next year had finally come.

Looking apprehensively around, our parents found us. We were reunited with Mum and Dad and our new brother. We

were a family at last. We were hugged and kissed and admired.
All I could think of to say was, "Mammy, Miss John say if you
want anything, you mus sen tell she." My little brother Bernie
said, "Ah we gat groundnuts."

I'm sorry to say that they teased us about our accents later.
So much that I became very embarrassed and conscious about
the way we spoke.

*Our language is fundamental to our perception of
ourselves,*
Our identity.
*Besides, you can't really tell Anancy stories in standard
English.*
*For years I couldn't tell a good joke or have a good belly
laugh.*
I became encased in a linguistic straitjacket.
*My language crept out embarrassingly when I felt under
pressure.*

                                        Yvonne James

REGISTER LETTER

Every end of month as sure as sun shine
Expecting and anticipating go start
Tantie go go down to George Town PO
Wait patiently in the heat.
We did expect a special letter,
With blue cross.

When the lucky day come
We go rejoice and celebrate
Buy up and nyam down the place

A temporary change of diet man
We go go down the village shop and buy up big.
Iced chicken back did taste sweet!
Who had time to chase fowl all over the place
And watch them fly pon roof top.
No tasty coconut oil in we food.
Pure lard oil man!
We had dollars!
Best of all we did eat plenty pallette, popsickles
And shaved ice with pink syrup.

One ting doh!
Me did still love me cornmeal porridge
And sweet cocoa tea with plenty celement!

We did indulge we self with tariari and tulung
Sugar cake drops and fudge
Saltfish go get a rest
We go eat beef instead
We did buy plenty sugar to make sugarwater
and lime juice

Shop mauby did taste real nice.
Breadfruit was poor people food man.
We go eat beef instead.

Who have time to bed down in river
And catch crayfish?
We na able let crab gundy bite we.
Smoke herring did make a pleasant change.

When all de money done!
We na just wait patiently for the next
Register letter.

Yvonne James

PARCEL

Layers of brown paper carefully wrapped,
Secured with strong string.
Million of stamps and big writing.
Survivor of ocean and storms,
Admired and circled
tentatively touched

Anticipating, wondering imagining.
What would unfold?
Carefully, eagerly unwrapped
Incredulous quantity.
Volume so small!

Bright picture books
Fairy tales and nursery rhymes,
Pink baby dolls with blue blinking eyes.
Big pretty frocks, big trousers, big shoes!
Exercise books, erasers and pencils
Panty and petticoat with lace.
Pretty ribbon, talc and alarm clock.
Almanac to show we snow.
Sweet smelling soap, pink and peach
all kind a shape and size.
Things like them me did wish me could eat!
Colourful windup tin toys.

Enchanting!
Magical!
Who needed Father Christmas?
Transistor radio with battery to join us across
the miles
Jigsaw puzzle and candy

Light up we face with smiles

Precious gifts
Carefully selected.
Testament of devotions and love
We the ones you left behind
Could not imagine the
hardship you find.

Yvonne James

EARLY DAYS

Bade me skin in sparkling river water.
Brush me teeth with arrowroot.
Oil me body with sweet coconut oil.
Grease and comb me hair and put in pretty ribbon.
Put on white blouse and blue skirt.
Me didn't even have to wear shoes.

Look through coconut branches at the clock in the
sky.
If we late is licks
Run down the hill.
Pelt cross the valley
Speed through dry river bed
Past cocoa dam into the school yard.
Just in time man.
Before the bell ring.
Line up for inspection.
All dem who na comb dem natty head
And clean dem dutty nails get wrap on the
knuckles with de ruler

I used to study me lessons and behave meself.
Practise me ABC on slate good good good
Write dem down in the book
That letter E did give me endless horrors
Me did fraid that big leather strap you see.
Brer Rabbit and de Tar Baby was me favourite story.

Me did love recess
Dry milk mixed with water did taste nice.
And the sweet dry biscuits did have a real special
taste.

Me tink de weevils dem did add vitamins
Bwoy dem bugs did taste sweet!

When de bell ring for twelve o'clock
You shadow did small small, til you could
stand up on um.
Me used to get confused with them meal time names.
Me sure me used to go home at twelve o'clock
for me breakfast.
Roast breadfruit and bulljow was finger licking sweet
man.
All that saltfish, coconut oil, lime juice, cucumber
and big, beefy tomato
Fruity trees did give me plenty desert.
Mango, custard apple and soursop

We used to stand up in the hill and look out to yonder
Emerald, turquoise and sapphire

And all the time me wonder
If somebody in St. Lucia a ponder.

The school garden was truly exotic
we did plant okra, christifine and balanjay.
I love that word balanjay

Me did have plenty of friend
A we use to play coop, hopscotch and brown
girl in the ring.
Glorianna is the only body who knew my special friend.

I did love Raymond!

Me did really love school

But me first day was a real nightmare
Me fall down
Bruise up me face and buss me bottom lip!

Yvonne James

MONICA MAHABIER

Monica was born in Jamaica and came to England
when she was a teenager. She enjoys writing and
reading her poetry. She would like to have a book
of her poetry published one day.

Halcyon Days

A kaleidoscope of colours, earthy smells
zigzag across my memory. The colourful memories
take me back to my childhood. Life on a farm
where I grew up in Jamaica. My house is on a hill.
Riding on uncle's bicycle fill me with glee!

Memories of red letter days
when I was young and carefree
chasing exquisite butterflies
and swimming in the sparkling, azure sea.

Auntie Elsie's voice lingers in my head,
"Honey bunch, drink up your milk,"
as she stood beside me in her flowery dress
with long, black hair that felt like silk.

Those halcyon days...they beckon me
pulling me through a tunnel, way back in time.
Nuggets of golden evening spent.....
Bombards my mind, leaving thoughts sublime.

I am ten years old and I live with my aunt and uncle in
Annatto Bay, Jamaica. We live on a farm, surrounded by
acres of sugarcane fields. As well as the farm, we also
have a spacious house with a veranda, situated on top of a hill.
Uncle is landed gentry - really! He supplies the town with
fresh milk from his dairy. Life is exciting here. There are animals
of all sorts. Some horses, black and brown ones and a large

number of bulls and cows. There is a chicken shack out in the backyard and we always check to see if the hens have laid any eggs. An assortment of other animals: sheep, cats and dogs meander around the compound. I feed the newborn lambs with a milk bottle because they don't have a mother. It's a delight to feed them. I feel a sense of awe at such times. There are also new born kittens and puppies. I have a puppy of my own. He is black and white, I call him 'Patchwork'. I spend many a happy hour playing with him.

UNCLE NABBY

Uncle Nabby is of medium height and slightly tubby. He has glossy black and straight hair, parted down the side and always neatly combed. He has a smooth brown complexion. He wears brightly coloured short-sleeve cotton shirts and knee-length shorts. Whenever he wears trousers they are held together at the bottom with two bicycle clips - making it easier for him to ride his bicycle. He sometimes wears an old wide-brimmed hat to protect his head from the sun.

Whenever he goes into town to see people he always takes me with him. I ride on the back of his bicycle - sometimes he walks and pushes me along. It is coming up to evening time and there is a cool breeze and an orange sunset lighting up the sky as we go past canefields where men are finishing the day's work. Uncle stops and chats amiably with them for a while. I always get some sugarcane to take home.

Life with Auntie Elsie and my uncle is always filled with wonder. My auntie suffers from epilepsy and at times she is not well. I feel quite sad for her. She has to have someone to stay with her all the time. Our family is big so there is always someone to see to her and us children. Uncle spends so much money taking her from one doctor to another, but there is no cure. He is very protective towards her.

BIRDSHOOTING

Sometimes Uncle takes us birdshooting and we have to wake up really early and set off for the woods. We take plenty of food and drinks. Uncle takes his long shotgun. My cousin Dorette, Margarite and 'Sonny boy", Auntie Elsie and my other relatives tramp through the forest. The trees are large and strong. There are cedar, guinep, mango, soursop and star apple trees. We stop and pick some fruits along the way. There are an array of splendid flowers and plants; catstail, poinsettia, hibiscus and bougainvillea. We try to catch butterflies flitting by.

I remember splashes of colours and the smell of the flowers. I was so happy to be alive, then.

Sonny Boy is older than us girls and he and my uncle walk in front while we tag along behind them. We skip over trenches and play games ' Miss Nellie's Blue Drawers". This was a game where we touched our palms together, clapped our hands and chanted:

> Miss Nellie's blue drawers drop off her
> Miss Nellie's cakes must sell.
> Who will buy dem? Dem bwoy.
> Where dem will get money? They will trust it.
> Go on Miss Nellie, trust dem.
> Trust dem Nellie, trust dem!

A variety of birds are flying around us. They included tiny ones called 'chi-chi' bird. There are also sparrows and 'red-tits', hawks and of course big black birds called 'John Crows'. When Uncle comes across the birds he wants, he points his shot gun, shoots them and they fall to the ground with a thud. Sonny Boy and Uncle gather wood and sticks, build a fire and roast the birds. The smell of them is so pungent that it makes our mouths water. We tear off the little legs and dip them in salt and pepper when they are ready. Then we sit around the fire talking and laughing. My relatives told stories about 'Brother Anansi' and 'duppy', sometimes called 'rolling calf'. A rolling calf is a mythical creature that supposedly comes out at night and walk around with a clanging noise. I feel afraid then.

After spending the day in the woods we return home exhausted. After a bath and a change of clothes we are refreshed. We have our bath in a cistern outside in the yard. The cistern is in front of the vegetable patch consisting of tomatoes, callaloo, fever grass, cirroci and pumpkin. There are yams, cassava and banana trees. We play hide and seek and chebby chase amongst the plants.

BEDTIME

My cousin Dorette and Margarite share my bedroom. It is a very large room situated at the front of the house. We have beds made out of board with mattresses on and brightly coloured bedspreads. Our bed has a mosquito net to prevent mosquitoes from eating us at night. We sing, dance and play with our toys before settling down. Out favourite activity is jumping into bed and playing 'catch' with a tiny ball we have. We play marbles and Jacks. There is a radio in our room and we fiddle with the dial and tune into country and western music - we even pick up the BBC World Service. Before we go to bed we have a cup of ovaltine or a big mug of fresh milk with an abundance of froth on top. After that Auntie comes and tucks the mosquito nets around our beds.

Those were the days, those happy days, those halcyon days - with my family on the farm, feeding the lambs, and playing with Patchwork, my puppy. It was a pleasure. Those frequent trips into the woods to go birdshooting - what an adventure. Best of all I liked riding along on my uncle's bicycle into town to see people. I would jump at the chance to go back in time, to live those halcyon days again!

                                        Monica Mahabier

VERNELLA FULLER

Vernella Fuller was born in St. Catherine, Jamaica, in 1956. She was raised by her maternal grandmother until she was twelve years old when she came to join her parents in England.

Vernella went to secondary school in south London, did her first degree at the University of Sussex, Masters degree at the Institute of Education, London University and her Post-Graduate teacher's certificate at Goldsmiths' College, London University. She has taught for nineteen years in secondary schools, further and higher education. She currently works part-time in an American Exchange University while doing a doctoral research on education and achievement of schoolchildren of African-Caribbean heritage.

Vernella has had two novels published to date: *Going Back Home* (1993 The Women's Press) and *Unlike Normal Women* (1996). She has also contributed to *Something to Savour: Food for thoughts from Women Writers* (1996) ed. Laurie Critchley and Helen Windrath. Vernella is currently writing a commissioned biography of a Jamaican public figure and working on a third novel.

Vernella has one thirteen-year-old daughter Alisha and is a foster parent to two teenage girls.

Leaving Aunt Bea

To this day Elizabeth does not know why everyone called her
Aunt Bea. There was no one to whom she was aunt but in the
church she was aunt where others were sisters, and she was
aunt in the District where others were Miss or Mrs. Her
three grandchildren called her Aunt Bea too. Only her daughter
called her Mamma. Elizabeth knew that because all the letters
that came from England began 'My dearest Mamma' and
sometimes 'My beloved Mamma'. Looking back, Elizabeth
sometimes wished that she had called her something else,
Granny or even Grandmother, but mostly she wished that she
had made up a special name for her, one that not even Wilbert
and May used. A name just for them, a name between them,
a pretty sing-song name that made old people envious and
young children smile.

Elizabeth did not have a name for her father either. She
does not remember her father leaving for England, just him
being there and then the picture of him on the trunk in Aunt
Bea's room. As she got older she wondered why she did not
have a proper name for him after he left, she would just refer
to him as my father. There seemed to her no real need for any
other name. The 'Papa' she had called him up to the age of
four when he had left seemed unreal, even unnecessary. Not
that she remembered calling him Papa, she just supposed she
had done, like all the children in the District whose father lived
with them.

Her sister May cried inconsolably when it was their mother's
turn to leave one year later, accusing someone in the car on
the way to the airport (Elizabeth could not remember who), of

being responsible for her mother leaving. Dry eyed, Elizabeth was thinking, *'Why is she crying when we have Aunt Bea?'* Elizabeth could not see then how there would be any difference in their lives with both their parents gone. The three of them had been born at home, on Aunt Bea's land. She had been her daughter's midwife as she was everyone's midwife in Blue Hills and surrounding Districts. Aunt Bea would never leave them. What more could her sister want? her five-year-old mind wondered.

Back home from the airport, Aunt Bea let the three children sleep in bed with her that night. She did not have the heart to usher each to separate beds. The next day Elizabeth heard her telling Sister Doris, the Deacon's wife, "Two of them kick the living daylight out of me in their sleep last night and the other one cry almost all night."

"Poor children. Still, they have you. Plenty children would give anything to be raised by you." She smiled with warmth. "To be sure, you are a balm to everyone, old and young."

"I wish I had the balm to ease the pain. I lose my one child and the children lose both their parents."

"Tough times driving our young people away. The Europeans' appetite to wreck our families still can't be satisfied."

"You right. You too right."

"That one stick on to you, eh?" Sister Doris said referring to Elizabeth who was skipping on her own in the yard.

"I know. It worry me for true. I think she will take it hard when her parents send for her to join them in England."

She paused for considerable time.

"And part of me will die forever when that day comes." Aunt Bea noticed too late that Elizabeth had stopped skipping and might have overheard her. "Go find the other two and play with them, Bethy."

They watched the little girl skulk off clutching her skipping rope.

Elizabeth was confused, her appetite for skipping gone. She had heard her grandmother only realising then that she was not to stay in Jamaica forever with her Aunt Bea. Crying she rushed to tell her sister who was reading in the shade on a bench behind the house. "If they send for me, I'm going to run away. I will never leave Aunt Bea."

"They are our parents. They will have to send for us," her older sister said.

Elizabeth flew into a rage, "Well, I won't go. I don't care if they are our parents or not."

"You shouldn't say that, it's wrong. You have to obey your parents."

"Well, I won't obey them and you only saying that because you don't like Aunt Bea like me." She cried the more. "I will die before I leave her and go to that nasty cold place." May tried to hold her but Elizabeth pinched her hard and ran off.

Their mother's picture went up next to their father's on the trunk. Smaller ones were kept in an album. Aunt Bea made them look at them every month. One year a picture of a baby girl came, a year later a baby boy, two years later another baby boy. Sisters and brothers they were reliably informed. Fortnightly letters with postal orders came with entreaties to good behaviour, hard work in school and information about their own lives in England - information that seemed to Elizabeth the same time after time; the cold, the name calling. It all seemed so hard to her, so pointless when they could be back in Jamaica.

One letter did not bring the usual news and enquiries. "Father divine, one of your brother dead," Aunt Bea shouted as she scanned and read the letter before gathering the children round to hear their part. She read again to herself then, "Your brother dead. What a shame, only three years old. Your mother said he had a bad stomach. She took him to the doctor, the doctor sent him home saying nothing wrong with him. He died as soon as they get home." She shook her head as she did when disbelieving.

"Your father wrote a bit in the letter too. He said your mother just sitting by the fire, crying and crying."

Elizabeth felt only the curiosity and dull ache she usually felt when reading in the Daily Gleaner that a child she did not know had died. The three of them went behind the house to play four-side-cricket, as often they did on Saturdays, with the Maxwell's children from the next yard.

"You think we should be playing ball when our brother is dead?" May said, squatting to keep wicket.

Elizabeth had just taken up her batting stance. Wilbert, the youngest of them, oblivious of the conversation and uncertain emotion, marked out his run, charged full speed, ball grasped as he imagined West Hall to hold his, bowled, uprooting and scattering his sister's stumps. Wilbert and his team were not to be persuaded that Elizabeth had been distracted.

"You're not playing for the West Indies yet you know," Elizabeth screamed, storming off to sit with the remainder of the team awaiting their return to bat. It did not take Wilbert long to dismiss them too. Elizabeth fielded half-heartedly when their time came, impatient for the game to end. She only played cricket to give her brother practice at bowling when he was not at school, or with friends further up the District, playing for real.

Later she asked Aunt Bea, "Why do you think I don't feel sad that my brother has died? Why don't I cry?" They were sitting alone. Wilbert was playing marbles with his friends in the yard. Elizabeth could see May in the distance sitting under the shade of the willow trees that fronted their seven-acre property, reading. Aunt Bea's eyes drifted to her too.

"I thought it wouldn't be long before you sister go back to her books. How you all persuaded her to play earlier?"

"I think she felt strange that our brother is dead and didn't know what to do."

Aunt Bea groaned and stretched out her hand and took her granddaughter's, rubbing it as she often did before kissing it and letting go. Elizabeth stretched out on the wicker chair and rested her head in Aunt Bea's lap. The full force of the sun had left the verandah, a cooling breeze came from the cluster of fruit trees and herbage that led to the weeping willows.

"Child, how you feel is how you suppose to feel. There can be no right or wrong way. All I can say is, if I had the power it wouldn't happen this way, with our family in that foreign place. Whoever heard anything like that? Doctor sent sick child home to die? If the child was over here, even in this District, I would find some herb or bush tea to boil up for him. You tell me what kind of doctor that?"

Elizabeth reached up and stroked Aunt Bea's face, pulled herself up and tried to unplait one of the two greying ropes of hair that fell to the sides of her grandmother's face. "Child, leave me hair alone. When you can plait it back you can undo it."

"I'm learning. No true?"

"You doing well dearheart." Aunt Bea sent her for the comb and coconut oil she extracted the day before. "I suppose I had better wash it now and let you get you practice. Go behind the house and cut some single bible."

Hair washed and rinsed Aunt Bea sat with the single bible conditioner in her hair awaiting the mandatory minutes before rinsing again.

"Bethy, what's on your mind?"

The girl, puzzled as always as to how her grandmother knew that she had something on her mind to ask her, said, "You won't let them take us from you, will you?"

Aunt Bea sighed heavily. "Dearheart, the cold would kill me before time. I'm too old to haul and pull up."

The tears came immediately to Elizabeth and no words of Aunt Bea could console. "I won't go without you. I am never going to leave you. Never." She cried over and over. In the end, hair caked over long with single bible, and with heavy heart, Aunt Bea ceased speaking, gathering her granddaughter to her, she rocked her gently, already part of her beginning to die.

Vernella Fuller

BEVERLEY CLARKE

I was born in Manchester, Jamaica. I like walking, reading,
writing and falling in love. I am an idealist and romantic
who would love to develop my own PR company. I love the
writings of Alice Walker, Jamaica Kincaid, the colour blue
and the man in my life.

Journey Through My Roots

I was born in Davyton, Manchester, Jamaica. Mammie said that I was a coronation baby and that the queen had visited Jamaica and given me a penny - a coronation coin. Looking back, I would like to take an emotional journey from London back to St. Thomas, where I spent most of my early childhood, and to Kingston where I departed to England at the age of seven. The journey is a visual and spiritual one that takes me back to images of my dearly beloved paternal grandmother and the landscape of St. Thomas. The people and the scenery are the utmost in my mind, and that is what holds meaning for me.

Sista Mammie, Mas Nate and Barty are some of the people I remember. Sista Mammie was my paternal grandmother. She cared for me and my brother Tommy when my mother left to join my father in England. Sista Mammie will always be beautiful to me spiritually and physically in life and in death. Both parents were blessed with beautiful mothers. Sista Mammie's husband was not our real grandfather. I think he was her second husband. Sista Mammie was a religious woman. I remember going to church with her. The congregation were all dressed in white. People spinning around in a trance, jumping up and touching the roof. The religion was Pocomania.

I can remember being told that I couldn't go to baptism the next morning unless I had clean shoes. At that time my Sunday best was a pair of white plimsolls, which Jamaicans called bugga, or crepsoles. That night I whitened my bugga and left them out to dry but in the morning when I opened my eyes unable to sleep with anticipation and excitement, I awoke to find my bugga still wet with morning dew. If my grandmother had found out she would clearly have stopped me from going from fear that I might catch my death of cold. My ploy was to stall by pretending that I was looking for something, allowing them to go on, so I wouldn't draw attention to my wet shoes. I waited until they were out of sight and then frantically drew on my shoes, pulled up my laces and tied them hastily. I rushed after them in the darkness of the dawn hills and down the valley from where the earth flattened out to meet the baptism procession all dressed in white on their way to the river.

Today I live in Southwark and every Sunday the Nigerians living opposite me dress in white and go to church. Their's is an alien religion to me but it shares so many similarities in dress with that of my grandmother's, maybe more. I don't share their language or cultural identity, even though I am an African and my grandmother also appeared to have practised the same religion in her own way. In some ways I feel sanctified. It makes me feel as though I am in a foreign country, seeing this. Although I have travelled decades in time, it's good to know that I am still close to my roots in the spirit of my grandmother and my ancestors.

My grandmother used to eat pepper straight from the tree. Another memory I have of her is the morning she went to empty her bedpan and a green lizard, the big one that can camouflage itself by changing colour, attacked her. Luckily my cousin Barty was around and was able to rescue her.

I loved the landscape of St. Thomas. My grandmother's house was detached on the flat of a hill that sloped down to the kitchen, behind the surrounding plantation were our neighbours. They were not visible, because the land was covered with citrus fruit trees around us; limes, lemons and oranges. Further down there were breadfruit trees, ackee and mango trees and a river. We used to catch fish from the river. We played on the hills, running up and down through the plantation and to the river. We had livestock such as pigs and cattle. The flat surfaces were more suitable for the cattle. We would see a mongoose now and then if we were lucky. We would walk miles before we eventually came to the river, passing maisonettes with balconies and surrounded by fertile vegetation.

We would fish for shrimps and crabs in the early hours of the morning. It was easy to go crab fishing when it was dark because the crabs couldn't see in the dark. Well that was my theory as a child and I'm sticking by it. You could put your hands over their backs and catch them that way.

Mas Nate was sista Mammie's husband and Barty's step-grandfather. Mas Nate was a cruel man. I can remember him beating my brother. I had to ride to school on the bare back of his horse while he sat on the saddle. Mas Nate wasn't liked by the local children either; I can remember when he was in the garden they would run past and call out 'flour head' because his head was as white as snow.

I went to two schools while I lived in St. Thomas. One was local. After finishing there I was sent to a school further away. I would be taken by horseback to school in the morning and sometimes I would walk home by myself afterwards if my grandfather was unable to collect me. The second was a government school in town and I was given dinner money. I had a choice of buying my lunch from the local shops or from the canteen. I can remember buying a fried dumpling only to discover that it was raw inside. I would also have school dinners. There was the compulsory milk powder which I relished like sherbets, but I didn't have a lollipop. I would use my finger instead to lick off the milk powder.

Barty was handsome. I can always remember him in a pink shirt with shiny, pink spots on. Barty's dad was in America and he got his clothes sent to him from abroad. My parents were also abroad and like Barty we were the envy of those around us because we got the best of everything. Majjie was my cousin. She and her mother would always open our parcels and try on my clothes, leaving me with the leftovers. Luckily for me she was fat and couldn't get into my clothes and my brother was lucky because he was the only boy.

I left St. Thomas to go to Kingston when my mother came for us from London. The St. Thomas of my childhood was hill and gully country. The urban landscape of Kingston was different from the country. There was hot tarmac, the concrete, the traffic and the lack of space with four or five houses and families in the same yard.

I met my new family for the first time in Kingston. My white step-father Tom, my two brothers Michael and Paul and sister Marlene, who was conceived in London, but born in Jamaica. My older brother was also called Tommy, so now there was a Tommy Junior and Tommy Senior. We lived for a year in Parry Road, Kingston in a house owned by the Johnson family, who later ended up in London.

Paul, my younger brother was called Castro because of his resemblance to Fidel Castro. Although he was only young, the women loved him and he loved them, especially the ones in shorts. I can remember Lola, the kind of woman you would see on Fifties postcards dressed in beach top and tight shorts. She was leggy and glamorous, like Dorothy Dandrige in 'Carmen'. My brother would innocently touch up her legs and everyone laughed at the forwardness of this child - as black people would say.

Though my mother spoke Patois, as a child I was not encouraged to speak it. I was forced to speak standard English. But, there are some stories which have to be told in the style of my mother tongue or else the whole point of the humour is lost.

My brother Michael was always caught with tomato juice dripping down his mouth but would always deny stealing the tomatoes.

"Michael did yu teif di tomato from the fridge?"

"No Mammy."

"Well how comes there's tomato juice running down yu mout?"

"I don't know Mammy!"

By this time the question and answer session turn to licks and Michael screaming out and crying, but no matter how much licks Michael got he still wouldn't admit to stealing de tomato. Everytime Michael get licks we would laugh and laugh. Amongst our family and friend it was an open secret that Michael was the tomato teif, although he never admitted to it.

Other events in the yard were the gossip about the incestuous relationship between a brother and a sister who were living together as husband and wife. Dogs were not treated as pets and were kept outside the house. Lizards were to be found everywhere. In fact you couldn't walk anywhere without shuffling through them. I wore shoes, but I also loved walking barefoot on the soft, hot tarmac in Kingston.

I remember living in Rhum Lane, Kingston with my mother and running indoors saying that rastaman was coming for me. To me, rastamen were like duppy, something to be frightened of. According to what grown-ups said, they were unacceptable.

My memories of Kingston also consisted of smells. The smells of different foods. Something I didn't associate with St. Thomas. There were always lorries full of ice and cups full of shave ice with syrup. The aroma of fresh cornbread being baked across the road, the taste of mackerel and green banana. The flavour of hot chocolate and Milo with vanilla, cinnamon and nutmeg; mint tea first thing in the morning to make you belch. Pardon! Shopping and getting free glasses in packets of Quaker oats. The milk jug with red tops and handles full of nestles condensed milk that we would pour out on hard-dough bread; or pour layers on our hands when mother wasn't around and licked it off in sheer ecstasy. This was what Kingston meant to me, home comforts, the smell of food, a clean house, clean clothes and my mother. That is why I remember Kingston so much. Kingston was where I lived with my mother, it was where I shared her, that's where I experienced her maternal security.

I found myself indirectly apologising for not loving my mother and feeling the need to justify my feelings about her. I do not have any emotional bonding with my mother, but what I have is an emotional bond with places. My mother provided the material comforts and I was never without anything. She was a good provider, but she did not nurture me, my grandmother did. Therefore I could never get close to my mother. African mothers share their children with the community, but the child always belongs to the mother, wherever she goes, however long she stays away, whenever she decides to come back. I have seen many examples of that and therefore I am inclined to relate my childhood experience to the African child rather than the western child.

In Jamaica children are never far from the adults, in the kitchen, at church, out watering the cows. They went everywhere. It is a child-centred society. I was a bit of a tomboy and a busy-body. I was always getting involved in big people's business. I guess I was brought up that way and didn't feel left out of anything. Up to now I don't know my place. I guess I never will.

My grandmother came to visit us when we came to England. It was a brave journey for her. She must have missed us to have travelled all that way to see us. We were wrenched away from her and I guessed it must have broken her heart. The emotional journey she made to see us to say goodbye before she returned to Jamaica will always stay with me. Sometimes, when I feel lost and alone, I go into the pit of my soul and try to reach her. I don't know if I succeed, but she was my first emotional bond, a bond that I have been unable to form with my natural mother. Years later, when my older brother Tommy had lost the will to live through alcoholism and a broken marriage, he mentioned Sista Mammie out of the blue. In all our years in England, I did not remember us sharing our childhood memories in Jamaica or ever mentioning Sista Mammie. It was then that I knew I would be allright and I could cry for joy. We were the two eldest and we shared something special as we were the only ones brought up by her.

In January 1977 I went on holiday to Jamaica. While staying at my uncle's home in St. Andrew we were paid a visit by a school friend of my mum's. My Uncle had phoned him to let him know that I was there from London. He had gone to school with my mother and had brought the house that I was born in. He had done it up and also bought a home in Kingston. He said he would only sell it to me and wasn't in any rush to sell; and I should let him know when I was ready to buy. My house is still waiting for me. One day I shall claim it.

Beverley Clarke

LEROY DEAKINS

Leroy is 43 years old. His dream is to return to his
place of birth in Jamaica and to 'settle down'.
His ambitions are to have his own business,
write a novel or film script. He also wants
to be a good Christian, and, most importantly,
to be totally happy.

Longing for Esther Piece

Ｍy mother abandoned me when I was three months old. As a child in Jamaica I would dream about her, and wondered what it would be like meeting and living with her. Even now, as a forty-three year old man, I missed my mother in those early years, and wish that I had been brought up by her.

Instead, I was brought up by my loving grandmother, who was called 'Auntie' by everyone who knew her. My grandmother gave me all the love and attention I needed as a child. Of all her grandchildren I was her favourite. She spoilt me because I was the son of her youngest son. I received more love from her than I ever got from my father or step-mother. I resented my stepmother when I was a child, because I thought she was trying to take the place of my real mother. I missed my real mother and craved her love.

By the time I came along my mother already had one child, my sister, by another man. She was then courted by my father.

My mother lived in her parents' home in a large village called Mattine. My father was from the neighbouring village called Esther Piece. He was the youngest son of my grandmother. When my mother was pregnant with me, her mother whom we called aunt, told my father to keep away from my mother and of course he ignored her. She was a cruel and vindictive woman and during the pregnancy she beat my mother constantly. She would hit her in the stomach with breadfruits the size of watermelons. It was a miracle that I was born a normal healthy baby. As a result of the treatment meted out to her, my mother abandoned me and that was how

I came to be living in Esther Piece with my grandmother.

Whilst still a baby I was looked after by my uncle who fed me on unsterilised cows' milk and left me sitting up for long periods, so I developed a life threatening back problem. I was very ill and had stopped feeding before I was taken to a doctor. The doctor told my grandmother that my spinal column had become separated at the lower back and I only had about a year to live. Everyone thought I was going to die, but my grandmother refused to give up and nursed me back to health. A friend of my grandmother, by the name of Bertie Small, who practised herbal medicine told her to feed me on certain roots and tonic. This I was fed on daily for about a year and that healed my spine. Some years later I was playing with a friend and he gave me a body scissor and this re-damaged my spine. Today, I still suffer with a bad back.

The village of Esther Piece consisted of the main shops, a Post Office and a rum bar. At the foot of the village there is a bridge over a river called Big River. I used to catch fish and swim in the river as a boy. Esther Piece is an old slave plantation village. There are twelve villages set up like this. They are all self-supporting. We grew: coffee beans, cocoa beans, bananas, yams, oranges, pineapples, breadfruits, mangoes, ackee, dasheen, callaloo, avocados, sweet potatoes, jackfruits, sousops, and sugarcane from which we made brown and wet sugar that we used to make rum and root wine. We sold these ground products to the government and to buyers called 'Higglers' who took these products to the big city of Kingston and Linstead market to sell for a living. My family on both sides also kept livestock. In fact my paternal grandfather bred race horses. He was also a vet and people called him the animal doctor.

In Esther Piece I grew up a shy child. I went to school and played mainly with my cousins. I was looked after by my Aunt Adlin or 'Tatta' as we called her. She taught me how to make coconut oil, by boiling the coconut cream until the water and cream evaporated and only pure oil remained. We also made drinking chocolate from pure cocoa beans.

When I was five I had my first sexual experience. I remember that one of my cousins tried to have sex with me. We were swimming in the river and she took me to a cave where she tried to put my penis inside her. I tried to do it but I was not sexually aware and my penis would not rise. She often played with my penis. This used to make me angry and I would cry and try to beat her up - but my feelings were mixed up because underneath the anger I really loved her. She was two to three years older than me and even now I still think of her. If I had known you could have married your cousin I would have married her. She was my girlfriend from the age of seven until I came to England at age eleven. Even though we were so young we had regular sex. I tended to mix with older children because I was sexually aware from an early age, and also more mentally advanced than children of my age. I was bullied a lot but I never liked hurting other children. I was very strong and active, but I was never cruel and I only fought when I had to. I had lots of friends and was the village hero due to my fighting skills. I wanted to be a world champion boxer. I was a strong, quick and aggressive fighter.

I came from Jamaica to the heart of the West Midlands to live with my natural father and my step-mother. They lived in a town called West Bromwich on the outskirts of Birmingham. They were very strict with me. From the age of eleven I had to cook and clean the house from top to bottom. My step-mother use to inspect the house when I had finished and if there was any dust I would get a beating. Any mistakes also got me another beating when my father came home. I was terrified of my father - but despite this I still remained a loving and obedient son. In fact you could say that I have forgiven them and put it down to their own strict upbringing.

My step-mother was herself mistreated. She had no children by my father so she was a bitter woman who was jealous of the bond I had with my father. She felt threatened by this, as I later came to understand when she told me the sad story of her early life. She had been brought up in a well-to-do old-fashioned Jamaican family by a very strict aunt. She got pregnant when she was only fourteen and was thrown out of the house with all her possessions and her baby. The baby was a boy which later died from neglect due to the unsheltered life she led.

In England I went to a very rough school and suffered a lot of racial prejudice. I was ill-treated at home and had to fight off bullies every day at schools. Needless to say I did not achieve much at school educationally. I was sent to church regularly on Sundays, as well as young people's meetings and bible studies on Saturdays. Neither of my parents were religious but going to church was a way of life. I use to go with my step-mother. I found religion quite overbearing and so I started to rebel against it and against my parents in my late teens. I started going to discos with my best friend. He taught me how to smoke and generally how to rebel. He was from a broken home. You could say I was led astray. We called ourselves the 'Original Disco Kids' and dressed up in the latest fashions of the seventies. - but we soon got targeted by the police and were locked up regularly. The first time I got locked up for assault was aged sixteen at a 'blues dance'. I got into a fight and was sent to a home for young offenders in 'need of control'. You could say that was the start of my downward spiral. After that I got involved in drinks and drugs, and now I am doing time - six and a half years for robbery.

I keep telling myself that if I had stayed with my grandmother I would have been allright. I wouldn't have ended up in prison. I always resented leaving my grandmother. She never beat me and I use to write to her and tell her about the abuse I was getting from my father and step-mother. I was depressed and unhappy but I never told her everything incase she got worried. I miss my grandmother . When she died she was 105 years old. I was broken-hearted. Part of me died with her. She was my best friend.

I am looking to a bright new future when I come out of prison. I have a loving beautiful daughter whom I called Leah, after my own name - Leroy. She reminds me of my grandmother and she has some of her strengths which compensates. I also have a loving girlfriend whom I've been with for sixteen years. My serious relationships have all been with white women and I realised now that was perhaps because of the treatment I received from my step-mother and my mother abandoning me at such an early age. This rejection probably put me off women of my own colour.

I used to get into a lot of trouble because I thought no one cared, now I know that they all care and want the best for me. My friends and family have all been very supportive of me in my long prison sentence.

I have met my mother again and since I have been locked away we have become very close. We were first reunited when I was ten years old - the year before I came to England. I remember that she took me for a day out to Maypen. I remember that it was very hot and we ate watermelons all day. She has never explained anything to me about her experience or why she abandoned me. I think it's too painful for her. She has become a born again Christian. I have told her that I don't have any resentment towards her. I just want to show her how much I love her and for her to love me. I want us to have a real mother and son relationship. I have even made peace with my father and my step-mother. For the first time, they hugged me.

My life in prison has not been wasted. I have educated

myself since being in prison. I have taken an NVQ in painting and decorating. I am learning to operate a computer and I am doing a Business Studies course because I want to start my own business when I am released. I want to be financially independent and secure. I want to prove that I can stand on my own two feet and my family have told me if I need any help they are there for me.

Like my mother I too have recently become a born again Christian. I now have a deep love for my family and an inner peace I've never had before. I love, value and respect myself. Through trusting and loving the Lord I have discovered the true me and can finally come to terms with myself.

I hope one day to go back to Jamaica and build a house in Esther Piece where I was brought up. I liked living in Esther Piece. Perhaps one day I will settle there again and marry a village girl.

Leroy Deakin

NATALIE SMITH

I live and work in London. I strive to write in an appealing and uplifting way to appeal to as many people as possible as I believe people largely like to be entertained when reading. I believe everyone has a story to tell and one day hope to write about my life in the Caribbean. I enjoy sunshine, thinking, and people who make me laugh.

...If Grandmother dies

Dear Mother,

Grandma nearly died last night. The pain took hold in the middle of the night and she never stop crying till this morning. All of us was so frightened we just hold onto one another and start to cry.

Glen and cousin Wilfred try to run next door to call Miss Vee but the dogs them start to bark and carry on bad, they run come back. And all the time they shouting for Miss Vee no one bother to wake up. All I could think to do was pray. The verandah was my altar as I kneeled down and asked God not to take my beloved Grandma.

Wilfred and Glen went out to the Kitchen to boil some strong herb tea while me and Lloyd rub bay rum and some other ointments all over Grandma's aching body. Thank Jesus, God listen to my prayer and spared her life.

What will happen to us if Grandma dies? We don't have any family here and Grandma is very old now. Though she loves us with all her heart I can see that we are a burden. Of course she don't complain but I can see she is tired and worried about us. She never say so but I know she wants you to take us, even though it will break her heart to see us go. I know you must be doing your best to save some money so we can join you in England but why is it taking so long? It's been eight years since you gone and I don't even know Father since he left before I was born.

Mother, even though I write you plenty times before it's the first time I express myself like this to you and it's all because of what hapened last night to Grandma. I suppose I never think of Grandma not being here before. I always think she going to be with us forever but last night really hit me hard. I thought I was going to have to send telegram for you and Father, to say Grandma dead, but luckily I am able to write instead.

Last week I overhear Grandma talking to sheself. She say she can't afford to keep us. She want to stop going to market every Wednesday and Friday night, but she can't because she has to support us; even though her body is tired she has to keep going. So you see mother this is why I am writing to you like this, to tell you what's really going on. I know you and Father think we always writing and asking for money, as you always write and ask us if we think money grow on tree. We know things must be hard in England, but it is even harder for us out here and poor Grandma shouldn't have to keep us.

You know the other day this boy tease me in school because Grandma beg his father for money and some food. I was upset and tell teacher and the boy had to say sorry but I was so ashamed because the boy said it in front of the whole class. The thing is he was telling the truth. Is not the first time that Grandma have to beg rich people for things and I know say people talk about us all the time. They say things like 'but those children have family a foreign and they don't have...it's a shame'. Nearly everyone round here poor so you know it's bad even the poor people talk bout you.

I hear say they don't have poor people in England. That's what everyone out here say. You know even though we don't have much the other children get jealous when they hear say we going to England soon. So when can we come, and can we bring Grandma with us? I think the others agree with me. Mind you this morning I tell Glen and Lloyd I was writing to you and asked them what they wanted me to tell you and Father and they just kissed their teeth. I don't think they care. They both say they haven't got any parents and Grandma is who they care about as she's the only parent they know. They also say they don't remember you, but I don't understand, they older than me, they should remember you. I remember you. I think so.

As you know I'm the brightest cause I always write. I always come first in my class and my teacher says I'll be even better when I get to England as their education is good. Is it true there are no dunce people over there? That's what I hear!

Grandma has just asked me what I am writing to you that is taking so long. Her voice is weak but she seems better now. I can't believe she is still here. I'm glad I prayed. I tell her I nearly finish but she don't know, I got plenty more to say. I didn't go to school today. I stayed with Grandma to make sure she allright. Everyone else has gone though. Funny how boys forget easily but Grandma says their education is more important. You know, we still don't know what was wrong with her and there's no one to tell us.

Last week she did write out a letter to you and Father but never post it. She not very good with words so that's why I always write for her, but I feel you should know what she write. It did say: Dear Mr and Mrs Barrett, is a long time since I hear from you, and even longer since I get a postal order. I am an old woman now and don't know how much longer I've got left. I'm finding it hard to look after your three children and their cousin as they can't live off water and fresh air alone. Cost of living gone up and the little money you send three months ago can't feed and clothe four growing children as you expect. If it was me alone I wouldn't ask for a thing but the children them have to eat. God Bless. Yours Truly, Millicent McIntyre.

I think she was vex when she write it but I can understand how she feel. Me, I'm different. I don't get vex like the others, although sometimes I do wonder if you forget about us and only care about our brother and sister in England. But, I know one day I'll come to England and join you. In fact the other day I dreamed I was over there with you, Father and my brother and sister. Lloyd and Glen weren't there. I don't know why that was... but anyway you had a big house, like those they have in the hills up in Kingston and three bad dogs to keep the thieves out. One thing though, you didn't have a face, and neither did Father. Isn't that funny. The whole dream was about you and you didn't have a face. There's a picture of you and Father in the cabinet. It's been there ever since I can remember so we don't take much notice of it now. I think it is suppose to remind us of you, but it's just a picture to me.

Some of the girls at school asked me what my mother looked like. I think of you in that picture looking slim and stylish and I told them that you had no teeth, one arm and a twisted face and that I would get you to frighten them if they didn't leave me alone. I don't know what made me do this. I thought it was funny but they believed me and haven't bothered me since. I hope you're not vexed that I said that.

Lloyd and Glen have just come back from school. They say to ask you for a pair of plimsoles and a cowboy outfit with guns and holsters. I ask them why they don't write you themselves if all they can do is ask for fool fool rubbish. I think they too lazy. Glen says girls should be the one to write but I don't agree. Still, I don't mind. It gives me a chance to tell you all that has happened to us.

Oh, I almost forgot to tell you. Glen received his scholarship exam results two days ago and he passed with credit. He can now go to a very good school in Kingston or Montego Bay. I don't think Grandma wanted me to tell you. She never want him to take the exam in the first place as she say if he pass he will just end up staying here in Jamaica and not go to England with the rest of us. Glen say he don't know if he wants to come anyway.

I know Father write before and tell him if he pass he better off staying out here. I never tell you this before, but Glen was so upset as he says this meant that Father never cared bout him and never wanted him to come to England at all. He could not understand how Father could want this for him. He cried so much, but then he say is only Grandma he love so he would make sure he pass. He say he would not come to England now, no matter what happen. He just want to get some help with his books and uniforms, when he decide which school he wants to go to.

Me, I can't wait to come. I hear so much about how it nice over there that I have to see it. Plus all my friends them going away somewhere like Kingston and Mandeville and I don't want to be left here by myself. Also, Grandma says I nearly twelve and turning into a big woman and she don't want no trouble on she hands. Can't think what she means, cause I never been no problem.

Your daughter
Hortense

Natalie Smith

CLAUDETTE WILLIAMS

I migrated from Heartease, St.Thomas in 1966 with my younger brother to join my parents in Brixton, London. Like so many other children from the Caribbean of immigrant parents, my school experience was not a happy one. However, I attended Dick Shepperd Girls School and through dogged determination and the support of my parents, left school with a few 'O' levels and went on to college. I later trained as a teacher at Furzedown Teacher Training College in Tooting and I have been in the job of education ever since. I remain committed to improving the education experiences of black and ethnic minority children by training teachers at the University of North London.
This is a job I really enjoy.

I find writing a very hard and lonely experience but because I have lots of ideas and share an experience that is not widely recorded (that of being a black Caribbean woman growing up and living in London), I write. In fact it's a long time now since I wrote a short story and need to get going on another one!
I live happily with no dogs or cats in Tottenham!

Invisible Mass of the Back Row

I stand in the middle of the room, surrounded by anxious faces. It is my turn to recite the day's lesson. The Inspector's ruler points to me.

"Stand up. Recite the adventures of Columbus. What was the date of Columbus' landing in Jamaica? What were the names of the ships? Why was he in the Caribbean?" My heart pounds. The heat of the morning sun, soaking through the galvanised roof, is magnified inside the schoolroom. The stench of fear is in everyone's nostrils. Something tells me that my days of hidden, disposed of, dispatched to the invisibility of the back row, are numbered. I stand up, my limbs shaking uncontrollably, sweat dripping from my armpits, my eyes inflamed. My belly aches. I am petrified. Words fail to come out. They are formed in my head, but my lips do not speak them. The Inspector's eyes pierce me through. They demand a response, demand to be respected and obeyed.

"What was Columbus doing here anyway?" The trapped words inside my head tumble out. The rebel inside me is alive. The schoolroom becomes even quieter, if that is possible.

"You in for it," Patricia, sitting next to where I stand shaking, mutters without moving her lips. I know she is speaking the truth. The Inspector's face is frozen. Miss Henderson, form six teacher, pounces with the ruler. Her face says she is sure she could not have heard what she thought she heard.

"What did you say Hortense?"

From I don't know where, a power surges through me. My fists clench. My teeth lock into each other. Miss Henderson reads challenge in my face. I stand still, not daring to say any more.

"What did you say?" she commands, challenging me to repeat my facetyness. And again it happens. Words gush out of my mouth. "Is what Columbus did want? Who invite him here?"

Before the last word had left my lips, the sharp sting of the ruler cracks my knuckles. Stupidly, I had left my clenched fist on the desk in front of me. The blow brings me back to the steam bath. Sweat now drips from my face, floods my armpits, drips from between my legs. I could kill this woman with her sharp pointed nose, mean eyes and frightened face. We cross eyes, and for an instant I see the fear which has trapped us in this renk, smelly room. Miss Henderson is afraid. She is as much afraid of the Inspector as I am. My brains, what brains I have left, are bouncing around in my skull, goading me on. I will get more of the ruler. It is written across Miss Henderson's wrinkled forehead. My life is at an end! At least in this school. If Miss Henderson does not kill me with this ruler, my aunt is sure to finish me off when she hears how I back-chat the Inspector and Teacher Henderson.

My parents are in England and living with my aunt is like walking a tight-rope. One little slip and I am big trouble. Dis look and smell like big trouble to me. The lunch bell echoes throughout the school. My salvation? For now, anyway.

Hungry bellies rumble in the steam bath, but we are still transfixed by the inspector, paralysed by Miss Henderson's stare. Feet shuffle, fingers scratch prickly skin. From outside there is the freedom of released bodies bouncing against the partition and liberated voices rising. They magnify our imprisonment. But the walls have been breached. The jailers are quick to realise that this battle is lost. For now.

"Class dismissed," the Inspector grudgingly commands. Miss Henderson lowers her eyes.

"Good afternoon, Inspector. Good afternoon, Miss Henderson," we recite. Miss Henderson steps aside, stiffly.

Fifty tense bodies scurry past, politely, straining to taste the
fresh, if hot air of the noon-day world and feed themselves
from the lunch women under the cotton tree. But first there is
Lorna Phillips to take care of. Somebody has to pay for this.

"Yu red pickney always sit a de front of de class. Unno
tink is because yu pretty. Is only cause teacher frighten fi yu
pupa," I curse Lorna, as we bundle down the steps, out of
earshot of Miss Henderson and the Inspector.

"Is cause yu black and stupid why teacher mek you sit a de
back all de time," Lorna chirps in.

"Is who you calling stupid? Yu want yu bloody nose right
here?"

This is always the outcome of tense morning in school. A
fight often follows the inspector's visit.

Lorna pushes past me and tries to make a break for the
school gate. But I give chase, followed by Samuel, Tim, Patricia,
Maud and Yvonne. Today she will pay for being teacher's
favourite, for being "red", for being rich, for having everything
I don't have.

"Look how fast she moving on dem marga foot," taunts
Yvonne.

"Come, let we beat her up," I shout, and we surge forward,
pursuing Lorna out of school. I might not know the answers,
but I can fight. Just then, from behind the school gate, Teacher
Edwards comes into view. He is big, sturdy and beautifully
dark, with a baby moustache. He is handsomely dressed in his
Dashiki suit. There is a kindness about this man that is not
usually found among teachers. He would always listen to you,
and not just take the teacher's side. He only beat you if he
really feel you was out of order, rude, or you get catch with
something you thief. We respected and even liked him.

The running stops, slows to a polite walk. The hot pursuits
melts into fixed grins and prim steps.

"Good afternoon, children."

"Good afternoon, Teacher Edwards," we still the vengeance in our voices long enough to chant unison.

Lorna makes the most of Teacher Edwards's presence.

Walking as fast as she could, she says a polite good afternoon and makes a beeline for the hill which distances her from the rest of us. She is safe this time. We turn down the hill.

"Mek she gone. We'll get her tomorrow," we plot. My voice and limbs quiten down. For the first time that day, my heartbeat falls back into its normal silent rhythm. There is always tomorrow.

It is the pain of the Inspector that has fuelled my blood; the pain of the ruler was nothing. Chu, mi use to beatings. One little ruler slap a nothing. But dat renking, facety man. A way him come from? Dis warra warra man, jus a bother people head. Him know de score. After all him is suppose to be black. My uncle say all dem collude to humiliate, not just me, but all a we, all de people who look like me. All de poor black people dem. Mek him no pick pan de red pickney dem, a mek him tink say is we alone no know nothing.

I walk silently down the hill with others. Each of us is distracted by our own thoughts and anger at the morning. Food hunger is temporarily forgotten. Lorna Phillips and de Inspector dem all de same. Have plenty of money and hate we.

At the bottom of the hill, we nourished by the wealth of warm, familiar sights and smells. The lunch women come into view. They are always there, big and strong, jutting out from the base of the towering cotton tree. Miss Ivy, as always, has on her red tie-head. In the afternoon sun, as she sits on her three-legged stool, it makes her face glow. Her food box is secured between her legs.

Aunt Dine always smells of cinnamon. You know her smell, because if you dare to make her laugh and expose her bare toothless black gums, in quiet moments she will give you a big smothering hug. Her missing teeth give her face a funny, quaint look. She is never scary to us because she lives in our districts and we know her.

Miss Mavis always sits to the right of Aunt Dine, because, she says, she is practising to be on the right- hand side of her Maker. Miss Mavis has the most beautifully oiled ivory coloured skin in the whole world, and white, white eyes which twinkle and wink at you when she talks. She is never cross for long, but will cuss you out one minute and tell you scriptures the next. Her face is electric, whirling and changing as she speaks. Her eyes search your face for understanding.

And then there is one-foot Herby who is always late with his sky-juice and snowball. He can argue, always on about de dam hot sun, which is good for nothing, and only melting him ice, quick, quick, o'clock.

The boxes are unwrapped. Our sense are assaulted by saltfish fritters, fried dumplings, red herring, cornmeal pudding, sweet potato pudding, oranges, plums, mangoes or sugar-cane, snowball and sky juice. Smells mingle and whirl, creating a comfortable oasis under the gigantic cotton tree. That same tree serves as a lovers's nest and gambling spot at nights. If trees could talk, what stories this one would tell!

We go down the hill. The gloom of humiliation, the pain of the assault on all of us, lifts. We search for our lunch money and think of food. Like swarming bees we descend, shouting our orders to the lunch women.

"Unny stop de noise and wait. How many han yu tink we have?" Miss Mavis quietly reprimands.

The shouts subside only for a moment as we change our orders and surge again.

"Two penny worth of dumpling and saltfish, please Miss Mavis."

"Mi only want one fritters."

"Mi jus want a piece of cornmeal pudding today."

"But Aunt Dine dat red herring so little bit."

"Yu have no crackers again Miss Ivy?"

"How come Herby tek so long fi shave de ice?"

The clutter and bustle carry on until the sweat is running down the women's face. Wash-rags, carried on shoulder like a uniform, mop brows, as they try to keep track of orders and change.

"Lord unno pickey is someting else. Unno gone like nobody no feed unno. Dem mus a wuk unno hard a school today."

The chatter waves and heaves. The banter and retort goes backwards and forward until the lunch money secured in pockets knotted in handkerchiefs has been spent for the day.

Boxes are empty. We mingle, swap and taste each other's purchases, eat, talk with mouths full. As we drift away, so do Aunt Mavis, Aunt Dine and Miss Ivy. Herby is the last to pack up and vacate the cotton tree. The forces have been spent for the day.

Will I one day move from the back row? Would I be let off from reciting the day's lesson, just once? Would it ever be my turn to sit at the front, and not have to answer the Inspector's questions?

The house is buzzing. A letter and a big, big parcel have arrived from England. 'Me mother sending for we. Me and me two brothers going to Englan. Me mumma and puppa send fi we. Dat will show Lorna Phillips. She have no people in Englan. Columbus can get lost. No more standing up in the middle of the class. No more lot, sweaty classroom. No more Teacher Henderson. No more Inspector. Me a go a Englan.'

November sixteenth. It is dark outside. Night creatures are going to sleep. Day animals still don't know it is time to wake up. Inside, the lamp is lit, casting its honey glow on our faces still dazed with sleep.

"Unno go ask, and put on unno clothes," Salna orders. Sleepily, we obey.

The sun is creeping over Easington hills, reflecting the honey glow inside. Its full powers are still waiting to wake up. I cannot drink any tea, cannot eat what is to be my last piece of hard-dough bread and butter. My stomach is tight. My jaws are refusing to chew on this familiar taste.

"If yu don't want de tea, lef it an go put on yu clothes. Dem all dey pon de chair, and don't mess up de hair," I am ordered again. I do as I am told. No time for back-chatting.

Now there is much coming and going. In the dim light of morning, not yet full awake, neighbours come to say farewell. They bring parting gifts of mangoes, and presents for relatives in England not seen or heard from in many years. Like a stranger, I greet my new clothes, gingerly feeling, inhaling the new clothes' smells. I try to work out which pieces to put on first without disturbing my newly crafted hairstyle. I dress in silence, only now beginning to fully realise. Today, my every action, in this dim morning light, is to be registered in the cosmos as my last in this familiar, tiny, two-roomed house.

We piled into the van just as the morning sun claims its place in the sky. It releases its passions and burns away the last stillness of the night. The silence of parting quiets the most active tongue. The drive to the airport is long and hot. Still, the pain of parting traps us in our silent world.

Who will look after Cousy's grave? Who will make sure that the weeds do not choke her roses? Cousy had not moved, as she always did, when the sun peeped over the hilltop. Had not roused me to do my morning chores when night kiss morning awake. I thought Cousy's coldness was just the passing night, so I slept on, not noticing that her "old bones", as she often referred to herself, had not stirred, that her limbs were stiff, that she got colder as the morning got warmer.

Lloyd banging on the door, ordering me to get up feed de chickens, alerted the yard. I woke to find Cousy's gentle face tight and still, a trickle of tears running from her open eyes.

"Why are you crying Cousy?" I asked as I crept sleepily out of bed. There was no reply. And I found myself crying too. Her stillness, her unfocused stare, signalled a change.

I opened the door to find the whole yard gathered outside, waiting. They understood the signals. Death had crept under the door and taken Cousy away in her sleep.

"I want Cousy," I hollered, as I fell into Miss Olive's arms.

Does this mean I won't ever again share Cousy's bed and snuggle into her warm bosom? Won't smell her old mysterious smells, and watch her crinkled face? Now, this thought forces out the hot salty tears which well up inside. I am leaving her behind. The stars flow freely, soiling my newly polished face. Bringing me back to the speeding van taking me away from Heartease, from Cousy, from my goats, from Lorna Phillps. Towards...the gigantic, shimmering aeroplanes.

The sun releases all its enormous strength. The sea retaliates. Its shimmers its bluest blue, a blue that envelopes the airport and the parked aeroplanes.

The following hours are filled with numbness. The only parallels I can think of are visits to the dentist with anaesthetics injected to deaden the pain or when you freshly buck you toe on a big rock-stone. My inside is dead. I am cold in the blazing sunshine.

Now, everybody is crying, some pretending that they aren't. Handkerchief flap goodbyes and wipe streaming eyes. My brothers and I are ceremoniously handed over to a pretty chocolate-coloured woman dressed in a blue uniform. We follow her, reluctantly, into places of strangeness, places with strange lights and strange demands. People smile knowingly and gather up your belongings.

Then we are sitting in the belly of the gigantic metal bird, which we have only seen before from the ground, looking upwards. This is it. We are going to England.

England brings my mother and father back to me. It drags them forward from the fragile recesses of my young memory. I remember snippets of incidents which had told me of their existence. How long have we been separated? Well, it is hard to know. It is hard, those days long ago, to understand what was going on. I cannot count how many days I was without my father's company, nor am I positive of the many years without my mother's embrace. But memory surges seven years perhaps, without father and five without mother.

I was not to know then that although I would return many times, that first departure was the beginning of my exile from Heartease.

Paraffin heaters
smell
always just coming
into cold dark places
afraid and
excited at the same
time
cold
smell
wanting to be elsewhere
in fact Jamaica.

"Yes, Salna," I replied for the tenth time, to my mother's call from the kitchen. A pokey, steamy place at the back of a cold, cold house.

All the houses I see are stuck together, with no place to play outside, no yard. Do children not play outside in this England? Is it always so cold? Does it ever get warm? Does the sun shine here?

"Now listen to me child," my mother's dark, youthful face smiles down at me, bring me back to the steamy place. I sit huddled in strange clothes, close to the paraffin heater. "You had better decide what you are going to call me. You can choose from Mother, Mummy, Mum. The same goes for yu father. You've got Dad, Daddy or Father to choose from."

This little talk put an end to days of nervous tension about deciding what to call my England parents. Having arrived, what do you call these newly acquired people? I dreaded answering to my mother's call. What do you answer when strangers call to you, but they are not strangers really, they are your mother and father? I fell back on old responses, familiar language.

No one told me I would need a new language in dis England.

"My mother who dey a England; my mother who a send fa me in a England." Here I was without a language to reply to her calls. Lorna Phillips, I still hate you, but oh I wish you were here. At least I know you name."

Mum came with me for an interview at Devon Spencer School. She sat right next to me as I read for the Headmistress. I read but did not know the words of this new language, could not read the words of this strange book. I did my best. I read until I was told to stop, being corrected by the Headmistress. The Headmistress was impressed. I was impressed. My Mum was impressed. My impressive reading enrolled me in one five, the hottest, baddest stream in the first year, only second to one six, the remedial stream.

My strategic location in one five has a familiar feel about it. There is no Lorna Phillips. In this group we have all recently arrived, from one island or another but mostly Jamaica and all poor, clearly black and one rung from the back row, the bottom stream. This is home away from home. I simply settle down to school life and cultivate the culture of the back row. We graduate in hair plaiting, make-up and cussing. Our section of the common room is dominated by the smell of hair pomander, face powder and Woolworth's latest perfume fragrances.

"You know say Columbus enslave de Indian dem fine in

the island. De same one of dem who save him life, and help him restock him ships and tell him say him no reach India yet." Jocelyn is feeding us information as she leafs through her latest book discovered at the local library.

"You lie!" The challenge comes from Fay Green. "Because is Africans dem enslave and ship to de islands, to slave on sugar plantations, fi make sugar fi white people tea in England."

The hair on the back of my neck stands up. The room is suddenly very hot. This man Columbus keeps coming back to haunt me.

"With all de tea dem drink in dis place, is we still a fe mek sugar fi sweeten it," says Jocelyn as she continues to leaf through the book, stopping every so often to throw out morsels about the exploits of slavers, life on plantations and the fights slave and the indigenous Indians waged for their freedom. Conversations weave and heave. We move back and forth between anger, total disbelief and downright outrage.

"Is who write dat book you reading? 'Cause is foolishness you telling me. I don't believe a word of it," Fay Green finally bursts out.

Each new piece of information is challenged and questioned. We discover heroes, rebels, guerilla fighters. They help us assert our rights to be. Toussaint L'Ouverture, Soujouner Truth, Nanny, Cudjoe, Paul Bogle. The book tells us they all come from our own back yard. Thoughts of them mingle with the hair oils, face powder, and self-affirmation lessons which claim space in our section of the common room.

Group humiliation replaces individual humiliation here in England schools. This bottom from remedial class gets the meanest, most feared teachers in the school. Their sole intention seems to be to ensure that we know and keep our place. And Columbus keeps coming up. Today's lesson is to make sure we have learnt the lesson of conquest.

Things mingle and whirl in my mind. Easington Heat.

Easington Sweat. English cold. English ice. Frozen faces, frozen information, frozen places.

Indignantly, the back row comes into its own. "Columbus was looking for a new route to India, so that when he landed in the Caribbean he was good and lost; he thought he was in India. The people who befriended him were massacred and the rest enslaved to mine gold and cultivate sugar. When they died from diseases Europeans brought to the islands, they were replaced by Africans stolen from the Gold coast of Africa, Miss."

I said all this slowly, so that I would say it well. Some of it came out just as I had read it in a book that some of the others had taken from the local library. Slowly, but quickly, because my head was hot and heavy. I can feel the others in the back row feeling proud. We watch the frozen faces thaw out. We watch her travel right along the two rows at the back. We watch a stream of red blood rush from the neck to the top of her head.

Fay Green cannot hold her voice back. "Hawkins traded trinkets for Black African people, who were enslaved and shipped to the Caribbean to slave on sugar plantations, to make sugar for English people's tea, Miss."

All eyes are on the teacher. The back row is tense, waiting for an explosion. The school pips signal the end of the lesson and class five, unusually dignified stands up and leaves the room, Miss remains fixed to her chair. Whoops and slaps are heard down the corridor. The back row claims a victory. "She won't be asking us those stupid questions again, will she?"

Voices are raised, claiming, proclaiming, learning the new language in dis here England.

Claudette Williams

Landing and Reunion

We were not dressed for the occasion, and were hardly invited, but turned up anyway. By the time we arrived, in brightly coloured party frocks and wafer thin shirts, the balloons had been popped and the drinks gone flat but the chill in the air signalled that we had arrived at the right place. Did they not realise that those willing workers that had come before would want to bring their offsprings as well?

First impressions last and it has stayed with many throughout their years here. 'Cold grey land,' 'freezing mornings', 'dark and foggy', are descriptions that crop up in pieces throughout this book. Coming from a climate with sky-blue waters, temperature where very little clothes were needed, England was the antithesis of home...but at least we had been warned.

Once immigration formalities had been dispensed with, strange women hugged wide-eyed children and asked even stranger questions like 'You miss me?' Hands were shook with new brothers and sisters and surroundings taken in.

Many of us expected to see the idyllic England of Christmas cards, of snow covered cottages in rural settings. Instead grey and drab buildings greeted us. It wasn't just people of the first generation who thought of factories on seeing smoke pouring from chimneys mounted on large blocks of flats, and were taken aback when they realised they were for living in. Certainly, the England of the greeting cards was there somewhere, but not for us.

Apart from these realisations, arriving on British soil sometimes had a bumpy landing. Ann-Marie Ellis' mother did not recognise her own child and their relationship went on to deteriorate from there; Judy Wellington was locked in a cell at the airport, strangely referred to as a 'place of safety'. In fact some people wondered who they were being sent to, as they had no idea. Iiola Ashundie described how she felt on this occasion in 'The Stone house'. "A man dressed in black came and said that he was my father. I stared at him in wonder. 'Is this my daddy?' my little mind asked."

The bosom of togetherness the children had hoped for that would help them overcome the lost years was often missing as parents expended little time on catching up with the past. Maybe they were too busy earning a living and had no time to mollycoddle their children who were in many instances treated as an extra pair of hands. Some existed with their family under the same roof as relative strangers. They were never able to bridge the gap.

Generally reunion appeared to have been uneventful and lacklustre. If parents threw a party to welcome children then everyone strangely forgot to mention that, there were no presents. The expectancy we left with seemed to have fizzled out over the ocean. Suffice to say the big occasion was no big deal for many arrivees.

The first few days were crucial. British ways had to be learned quickly. Even for parents with their permanent Caribbean twang, our raw accents was often a sources of amusement. As a result we became conscious of the way we spoke, knowing we must lose the accent to fit in. Though black children born here had their own form of 'West Indian' talk, it wasn't the same when it came to the real thing.

Living standards in the '60s and '70s of course were vastly inferior to that of today. Children arriving at the time would have been surprised to find the fairytale imagination they had of the good life was not the case. Mostly, families occupied two rooms in overcrowded shared houses, and facilities such as bathrooms were shared with other families. Unlike the Caribbean, where outdoor space allowed freedom of movement, England was restrictive and cramped. The great outdoors was no longer at liberty and we saw that people kept to themselves.

For the first time, many of us realised what our parents did to acquire the 'postal order' we craved back home. Believing they had important jobs we quickly fathomed that they were no more than second class citizens, working several shifts (and therefore rarely having time for their children) in order to keep a home and pay bills.

Despite the disappointments, we knew we were better off in some strange way. We were re-united with family members and that had to be good. Any negative feelings had to be forgotten, and, as before, we had to make the best of our situation.

JUDY WELLINGTON

Judy is a 48-year-old Adult Education teacher. She enjoys cooking, travelling and listening to the rain in the morning when she is warm in bed. Her dislikes are insincerity, back-biting and people who don't say what they mean. Amongst her favourite books are Toni Morrison's *Beloved* and Zora Neal Hurston's *Their Eyes Were Watching God*. Her aim is to be able to retire by the age of 60, continue to travel and preach the word of God.

Welcome to Britain

The last time I saw my mother she was dressed in a dull, grey suit, waving goodbye to me as she boarded a small schooner. She was on her way to an ocean liner that was docked further in the horizon and which would take her to England.

It was six years later when I travelled from Barbados to join her, my younger brother and step-dad. The voyage was the culmination of weeks of planning, shopping trips to town and lots of tears. I was leaving behind my wonderful grand-parents, whose overwhelming love and care had eased my heartache of Mother leaving. I do not remember how long it took before that heartache subsided, as I was only five years old.

As the years passed, her presence was replaced by a letter, every two weeks. Mother always wrote a few lines directly to my sister and me which grandmother read to us and made sure that she was always kept informed of our progress. Other letters were often sent too. These were crossed with a blue crayon and they made my grandmother very happy. Such letters contained 'postal orders', which had to be signed for before they could be cashed.

These letters also made me happy. They meant I could go into town with 'Mammy' (grandma), buy lots of shopping and have lunch before going home. During the weeks leading up to my departure there had been many such trips to Bridgetown. However, it was not in preparation for my journey to England. That came out of the blue. I had won a scholarship to one of the best schools in the island and had been to town to shop for books and uniforms.

It was fate that changed the course of my life. Amid the excitement of winning the scholarship, and the hope of travelling into town to school, I fell over while running and damaged my left eye.

I was taken to see an eye specialist who recommended an operation which would be best carried out in England or America to ensure success. My fate was sealed. New preparations were hurriedly made for my journey to England.

So in September, while friends were starting their high school experience, I left the security of my grandparents' love, and my familiar surroundings, to travel to England. Saying goodbye to my grandfather was the most difficult and painful moment of my life. He did not wish to travel to the airport so we said goodbye with him sitting in his rocking chair. I left with the promise that if I did not like England I would return to him. I held onto that thought, and gained the strength to leave.

My 'Mammy' said goodbye to me at the airport, assuring me that I "would be allright in Jesus' name". I did not see her cry much, but she was biting on her bottom lip, and I knew she was holding everything inside.

The journey to England took us to New York, where we changed flights. I can still vividly remember the beautiful sights of millions of light beneath me, as the plane began its descent into New York. It was a stark contrast to my grandfather having to pay for the electricity company to install a light pole in our street so that we could get access to electricity.

The airport was buzzing with people. It was my first experience of seeing so many, mainly white people in one setting. Another sight I especially remember were the telephones, there were so many, much more than I could have ever imagined existed.

I arrived at Gatwick airport, where I was due to be met by

my mother. But unknown to me, there was some confusion in the arrangement plans and my mother was waiting at Victoria Station.

As time passed and no one showed up to collect me, I was finally handed over to the immigration authorities. I provided the officer in charge with details on my mother and her address so that they could contact her. However, the officer chose to disregard the latter information, peculiarly believing that as a young child who had just arrived in Britain I could not know of an address here.

I felt a sense of indignation. Back home I had always collected my mother's letters from the postman. Before taking them to 'Mammy' I always made sure they were from Mother and not from other family abroad, therefore her address was printed in my memory. Also, I was used to memorising and reciting scripts and poetry in Sunday School, yet this officer was choosing to ignore the information I had given him.

The officer went off duty and I was eventually taken to 'a place of safety', which turned out to be a cell somewhere at the airport. I was not aware of my situation for a very long time, but gradually I noticed that there were bars around me and that the door was locked. It was also getting cold and I was not dressed for the weather in my pink, nylon dress, short, white socks and black, patent shoes. I can remember a distinct feeling of tension enveloping my whole body.

It was some time before a voice asked, "Do you wanna cup of tea luv?" I looked up to see a man in a policeman's uniform. He brought me tea, which tasted awful. There was no sugar and it was too strong. I began to cry. I wanted to go back to my 'mammy' and 'daddy'.

The policemen listened to my story and asked some questions. I told him everything particularly the fact that I knew where my mother lived.

I later found out that he contacted the local station and a

police officer was sent to the address I gave. Luckily, my step-dad was at home and my mother was located.

I sat in the waiting room, not aware that my mother would soon be collecting me. Suddenly I felt my body being squashed by a bulk, wearing a turquoise and black dress. I did not see her, but a voice said, 'Don't tink I did this on purpose. I was waiting at Victoria Station.' I kept silent. My joy gone from having being treated in such an inhumane way while waiting to be collected.

We travelled back on the train. My mother was talking to her husband about the length of time she had been waiting for me and how hungry she was. He explained how tired he was and that he had to leave the baby with someone else in order to locate her, after the police had arrived at the house.

They had both had a hard time of everything. I remember looking out at the darkness of the tall buildings. I still had not said a word and no one thought of talking to me. The conversation between them continued until we reached the place which was to be my home. I did not look into my mother's face. I was not able to speak to her husband. I had something to eat and went to bed.

Judy Wellington

ANN-MARIE ELLIS

Ann-Marie currently works part-time for a local authority in
the health and safety field. She has worked in this field for
over fifteen years and for a number of organisations. She is
a very ambitious person who believes in creating her own
destiny, instead of sitting back and hoping for the best.
As far back as she can remember she has always
loved writing, and English composition was her best
subject at school. She uses poetry to express her
true feelings but so far has not wished to publish her
poems. Ann-Marie is an Aquarian. She describes
herself as very confident, independent, romantic;
a true and reliable individual.

Shine Eye Gal

I remember that there was a lot of excitement and fuss in the days leading up to my departure from Jamaica. New clothes were bought. Cases were packed, and neighbours, relatives and close friends of all persuasions visited. The grown-ups chatted to each other whilst the children played together. I had no real comprehension of the journey I was about to undertake.

On the day of departure I was dressed up in a blue, frilly dress. On the way to the airport in Kingston I was sick and threw up all over the dress. After being washed and changed, someone gave me a nutmeg and told me to suck on it during the flight if I became air-sick. Fortunately I did not need the nutmeg, but I always remember that piece of advice even though I can't remember who gave it to me. I don't know whether the sickness was as a result of travelling or merely a nervous apprehension of leaving the country and people who knew and loved me to undertake a journey to a new country, and a mother whom I did not know.

I was not alone on my journey. I travelled with my sister Carole who is four years my senior. I did not know her until I was four years of age when I was taken to live with my step-father (Carole's father) and his family. Carole and I quickly became close friends. We were the 'black sheep' of this new family that I was dropped into. Everyone referred to us as Daddy's illegitimate daughters. I thought that Carole and my step-father were white. In my child's eyes they were so much lighter than me in complexion and it was not until I got older that I realised they were not white.

In Jamaica I was nicknamed 'Pattoo' or 'Shine Eye Gal' because I had bright eyes. On my arrival in England my big, bright eyes were suddenly bombarded and bewildered by a lot of strange new sights at the airport.

At the airport, I stood with Carole and some other children waiting to be collected. Suddenly a woman approached Carole smiling. She wore black gloves and was snuggled up in a long, dark coat. My nostrils were filled with the pleasant, sweet smell of her perfume. The smell was pleasing to me.

The woman kissed my sister. She then did likewise to another little girl who was standing next to us. I thought: how strange that this woman knows Carole and a stranger but not me. As these thoughts ran through my mind I heard Carole say, "Mother, Ann-Marie is here!" and pointed at me. I was now very confused. The woman was my mother but she did not know me.

That first meeting with my mother will always remain painful for me. The memories flood back easily and so does the pain. My mother did not recognise her own daughter. Yet that was the reason for my journey to England, to live with my beloved mother.

I had been only six months old when my mother left Jamaica in 1961 intending to improve her fortunes in Britain. She left me with her mother and it was to be another six years before I would see her again. In that time I had not imagined what my mother looked liked. I had no visual memory of her, and now to my horror here she was greeting someone else's child, a total stranger - whilst her own daughter the 'little shine eyed gal' looked on in tears.

On realising her mistake my mother eventually greeted me, but I don't recall how it felt, as everything lost its meaning. My mind went blank. I went numb all over and nothing else mattered. We drove home in silence. That's how it seemed. I am sure there was some conversation but I can't remember.

My mother spoke a lot, but saying what I don't know. I remember being given some grapes in the car. That was a new experience. I had never had grapes before. I liked the taste.

In England I discovered that I had four other siblings. I was introduced to my half-sisters and brothers. They asked a lot of questions.

"Who are you?"

"What are you doing here?"

"Where are you going to stay?"

"Where did you come from?"

"What's it like there?"

"What did you do there?"

All these questions had to be taken in my stride and answered. I felt like an alien, a stranger, surrounded by new faces in a new world. Having Carole meant that at least I had someone to stay close to whenever I felt insecure. We chatted about Daddy and the rest of the family that we had left behind. We wondered what they were doing back home and why they had not sent us any letters. We wondered whether they had forgotten us now that we were out of sight. In the end Carole and I concluded that we had each other and nothing else mattered.

The relationship with my mother was a non-starter. Looking back now, I realised that my mother fitted perfectly the stereotypical image of a harassed single mother. She always worked but was unable to be financially stable on the low salary of a trainee nurse; so she gave up her ambitions and became a bus conductress. I seemed to be forever babysitting, but I was not allowed to chastise my English born siblings in any way and would be beaten if I dared to offend them.

"A wha you hit dem fa?" Mother would scream as she reined down hits on my body. I always had to do some kind of housework such as the cooking or cleaning the floor before I would be allowed to eat. I was never paid, not that I wanted to be, but I wished that I had been praised for my assistance. Instead, I felt I was being made to work for my living and my mother took every opportunity to make me feel guilty about how hard she had worked to save the money in order to bring me to England.

"I lived on beans and toast," she told me, expecting me to show more gratitude. At times, I thought I saw hate in her eyes whenever she looked at me. I was never hugged or kissed by my mother. I could not understand why she had sent for me if I was so obviously a burden to her.

Whilst preparing to leave Jamaica, my step-father had told me that I was not to eat if I was not allowed to write to him and let him know how I was settling in. He was probably only joking, but at age six I took the advice seriously. I wanted to write to him to let him know that I was not happy, but I did not know how to go about it. At age six I did not know how to write a letter and even if I did, I had no access to pen, paper, postage stamp and neither did I know the postal address. I did not have the means to communicate with my step-father so naively I resorted to his advice to 'not eat'. My attempts to not eat proved futile as my mother just forced food into my mouth and I had to swallow or be beaten. It proved easier to swallow.

I soon began to realise that I was different. I was treated differently to the other siblings, including Carole. It was then that I realised that Carole was only my half-sister. It took over twenty years before my step-father confirmed to me that he was not my biological father. I took on the mantle that my paternity was a dreadful secret and that accounted for the treatment which I received form my mother.

Over time it became easy to play the game and not to challenge anything my mother said or did. I became compliant.

I did what I was told and avoided unnecessary contact with her. Occasionally I would sit and watch the television with my brothers and sisters , but as soon as I heard the rattle of her keys in the door I would retreat to my shared bedroom.

As I got older, I turned to my schooling and books for comfort. I got praised by some of my teachers and worked hard at my subjects. Consequently, I was the only one of my mother's children to leave school with several 'O' and 'A' Levels and proceeded to do a degree at age nineteen.

Now aged thirty-six, I am the proud mother of a seventeen-month old daughter. I had put off having a child because I wanted to be certain in my mind that I would be a good mother to my child. I do not want to perpetuate my mother's legacy of beatings or to lack physical contact with my child. A mother to me is someone to trust and feel secure with. My mother did not fulfil that image. I therefore suffocated my maternal instinct until I knew I could give my child the best.

Today my relationship with Carole is the strongest I have with any member of my family. My relationship with my other siblings is quite tenuous but I do not blame them for anything. My mother and I speak to each other out of courtesy and I respect the fact that she is my mother. I am always there for her, but there is no love. I don't even think we like each other. There are too many secrets and negative memories.

I have been asking my mother the same question for many years - the question of my paternity and I am still waiting for the answer. She always side-steps the issue. Her typical replies have been:

"Why are you asking me that?"

"Who told you so?"

"Just because your step-father is lighter, it doesn't mean he's not your father." It was only when I took the extreme action of not speaking to her for three years that she admitted that my step-father was indeed not my biological father. Her revelation was not a surprise because I already knew. I was only looking for confirmation. Eventually it came but it added no comfort to my pain because of the effort I had to make in order to acquire this confession.

There are still things I would like to know about my biological father. Things my mother believe are her business but which concern me as well. I believe I have the right to know because they are still directly affecting the quality of my life. Others know but I don't. Mother refuses to reveal the truth and so the identity of my father still remains a mystery to me.

Ann-Marie Ellis

IIOLA ASHUNDIE

Iiola spent her early childhood growing up in Basseterre,
St.Kitts. She came to England at the age of seven, where
she grew up in Luton, Bedfordshire. She is a single mother
of three, and her writings are based on her experience of
being abandoned by her natural mother and being posted off
to an unknown father and step-mother.

Iiola took her Masters Degree in creative writing at Bath
Spa University College.
She has taught literacy and creative writing and
co-founded Nka Iban Writers' Group.

Her writings can be found in *Sojourn* (1988) *Daughters of
Africa* (1992) *Words of Nka Iban* (1995) and
The Memory Bird Anthology (1996). Her play *Ngozi*
is waiting to be staged. She has also written a number of
yet to be published novels. Iiola is currently working on
establishing a publishing company with other members of
her writers' group. She is also pursuing a PhD in
contemporary Caribbean literature and creative writing.

The Stone House

THE BOAT

On the slippery steps of the boat I was hoisted up by a sailorman dressed in white. I landed on the deck of the boat which was heading for England. I did not know what day or time I left the home of my birth in St. Kitts. I was seven years old when I was packed off by my mother to an unknown father in England.

The boat sailed away from the land of my birth. The journey was long. It seemed like a hundred years. There was a woman who met me on the boat. She was suppose to be my guide and travelling companion. Her name was Miss Nesbit. I had never seen her before. Straight away Miss Nesbit began to abuse me.

One day the captain of the boat asked for some children to put on some entertainment. I was excited and wanted to join in the excitement. Miss Nesbit went crazy and dragged me away from the other children. Reaching the cabin she peppered my arse with licks, locked me up and went about her business. This was one of my earliest recollection of being locked away from society.

The boat came into dock en route. I don't know where. I was still locked up in the cabin and Miss Nesbit didn't give a damn. Nobody heard my cries or seemed to care about this small child. Looking out of the porthole window, I saw lots of people walking about. I started to wave at the people below. Some sailormen saw me and began throwing lots of money up to me. I thought if I could only catch a sixpence, then I'd be very happy. I couldn't catch any of the money and I just watched them slosh and disappear in the oily, murky water below.

The boat rocked to and fro, causing my belly to erupt into a volcanic bile. It felt like I spilt my internal organs in a face basin which was sticking out of the wall in the cabin.

One day Miss Nesbit had just finished tidying herself. Suddenly she flung her dirty, disgusting towel in my face, and then proceeded to enter my suitcase. She took out my nice, clean towel, which had the same colour and pattern as hers. It was turquoise and white.

"It's mine!" I screamed out.

I tugged and she pulled. I fought and she fought.

"You're not suppose to use my things." She didn't care. She peppered my arse with licks and locked me in the cabin again. This went on until the boat arrived in England.

There were hundreds of people at the port when I arrived. Coming off the boat the first thing that hit me was the cold. I shivered and placed a 'kerchief around my neck. The boat hooted loudly, throwing smoke out of its big funnel. Everything looked dull and gloomy. I couldn't tell whether it was morning or evening. Everybody was wearing black. I thought they were going to a funeral. In St.Kitts the only people who wore black were the people who marched up and down the streets on Sundays, blowing their boogle and singing the Lords prayer and wailing for salvation in high pitch voices. They frightened the life out of me. I thought the end of the world was coming. The other people who wore black were mourners who cried loudly when somebody died. When this happened it was the custom to throw dirt on the head and cry out. The dock looked and felt like a cold graveyard. I don't know how long I waited at the dock with Miss Nesbit, it seemed like ages. People walked around with sad expressions on their faces. They didn't seem to notice me. I don't remember Miss Nesbit talking to me, or reassuring me about anything.

THE FATHER

A man dressed in black came over and said that he was my father. I stared in wonder. He was a total stranger to me. 'Is this my daddy?' my little mind asked. The guide handed me over to him and he smiled and then took my little hand in his. We walked away from the dock and we passed some shops. The dummy in the shops frightened me. I had never seen anything like it in my whole life. I saw a doll in a shop window and I wanted one. The father said that he had a dolly for me at home to play with. I was so excited because I was going to get a new dolly. Then I wondered where home was, because mine was down the alley at Thibou Avenue in St. Kitts.

We boarded a train to a place called Slough. We entered a stone house and the father showed me his little baby. This was the dolly he had in mind for me at home. He probably thought I didn't know the difference between a dolly and a nine-month old baby. I was very disappointed because the father had lied to me and I'd only just met him. This was the start of a long nightmare.

He placed me in front of a strange woman. I'd never seen her before. He told me that I had to call her mother. I shook my head in dismay and told him that I was not going to call her mother. Her face oozed with hatred as she glared at me. The dirty looks she gave me sent shivers down my spine. I yelled that I didn't like her, but the father just brushed aside my emotions.

CANCAN

I was excited when the father showed me lots of crispy can-can frocks which he had bought me. There were pink ones, yellow ones and blue ones. There were plenty of nice, white socks, panties, vest and new shoes. I threw the shoes aside because they bun my foot and I couldn't walk in them. Back home I was used to going bare feet, but the father forced me to wear the shoes. This I did reluctantly, because this was England and people wore shoes.

The father treated me like a wild animal from the bush that had to be trained and tamed. I started sucking my finger and pissing the bed. The bed I had to sleep on was uncomfortable. I was so used to sleeping on the floor back home. One night there was thunder and lightening and I was frightened. I got out of bed and pulled all the sheeting onto the floor so I could hide from the thunder. The father beat me. The more he beat the more I wet the bed. The more I sucked my finger, the more he beat me. He put poison liquid on my finger. I sucked it off. He put black pepper on it. I sucked it off. He put shit on it. I sucked it off and cried for mummy. I wanted to go home. I was living in a supposedly civilized country, but no one came to help me.

In the day the father went to a place called 'wuk'. He left me with the woman. She feasted on my flesh all day. She told lies to my father. When he came home I got more licks. One day she had to take her chile to see a doctor. She didn't have any patience with me that morning. I was in my panty and vest and she blasted my arse with licks and locked me in the house all alone - bawling. I was alone in the house. I fought to get out of the house and find the father. I had no clothes on, so I took my yellow cancan dress and put it on. I opened the glass window and ran down the street still bawling my head off. I had no shoes on and my cancan dress was undone. A man who knew my father saw my distress and asked me what the matter was and I told him. He shook his head and went and found the factory where the father worked and left me with him.

I had not started school as yet so I stayed in the stone

house most of the time. I was fascinated by Bill and Ben the
flower pot men on a thing they called the television. I was
amazed to see these two strange flower pots dancing. They
made a strange *blobob blobob* sound. I went round to the
back of the television to see where they came from. I just
could not figure it out. I stared in wonder. The father hardly
spoke to me and neither did the woman. The woman use to
take me to a place called the launderette. She put Lux in a
machine which spinned, soaped and foamed. I was
mesmerised.

THE COLOUR RED

The father began trying to teach me to read and write. I could
read and write perfectly well before I arrived in England. One
day he gave me some sums to do and I was sitting at the table
doing them. There were ten all together. I did most of them
except the two that I didn't understand. I told the father that I
didn't know how to do them. His face exploded with rage. He
took his thick leather belt from around his waist and battered
me to kingdom come. How I hated the father. I came to the
conclusion that the father was evil. He was not human. I
wanted to take the boat and go back to Thibou Avenue where
I was happy once.

   I started school and became friends with - a bruk foot white
gal with wire in she mout'. I wondered how she got wire in
she mout' and why she walked with two sticks. She had a
hard white cloth on her leg. Nobody told me it was called a
plaster. The gal became my shadow. The teacher told everybody I had arrived from a different country and they were
fascinated by me. The bruk foot gal was intrigued by my dark
complexion, and she kept putting she hand in me hair. She
stuck to me like glue.

When lunch time came, they put grass on my plate to eat. I was shocked because this was the first time I had seen people eat grass. In St.Kitts, only pigs, cows and goats eat grass. I didn't know that this thing was called cress. I really like the bruk foot gal. She became my best friend. The father use to take me to the park to play with her. Soon, the broom and washing up plates became more important in the house than reading books and playing. The step-mother couldn't bear to see me enjoying myself with a book in my hand. I was labelled stupid and dunce but I knew I wasn't. I wanted to be a doctor when I grew up.

One day the father said that I had to change my surname. Up until then I had used my mother's surname, given to me at birth. I'd had it for seven years, so I couldn't understand why I had to change it. It was the name I'd written in my passport in joined up handwriting myself. Then the so-called mother came over and shoved it under my nose - the passport - which had a picture of my face in but I didn't even remember taking it. They had changed my name. It took me a long time to figure out and get used to the new surname.

I don't know how long I had been in England - when the father and the step-mother said that they were getting married and I was to be a bridesmaid. They got married in a place called Southhall. I remember there were lots of people in the house. A couple of days before the woman put on she white frock, she called me to come and look for she chile shoes. I looked high and low and couldn't find it. I told her that I couldn't find the shoes. Without uttering a single word, she reached under the bed and took out a spiky stiletto heel shoe and walloped me. The woman busted my head open. I screamed at the top of my voice. Blood gushed down my face like a river. Everything around me went black. The father came running into the room, and I screamed that the woman had hit me, because I couldn't find she chile's shoes.

The bath was red with blood. I bawled and bawled and the blood carried on running. It did not stop. No one took me to the hospital. The father went ahead and married the woman. She became my evil step-mother.

Ever since that incident I've always had bad headaches. The sight of the blood, makes red a colour which always brings bad memories to me. For years I could never wear red clothes. Gradually over the years I can just about tolerate the colour red.

Iiola Ashundie

The Breadfruit Tree

You were rooted in the earth on an island so far away
Your heavy green leaves sheltered me from the hot sun
I remembered when we grew together in the seven moons
of my youth
Shadowing me with your special gift

When the hurricane storm came
Your special fruit fell to the ground with a thud
Sometimes crashing on a tin roof below
And you'd become precious food to all who passed by

I watched you from the backyard
Camouflaging the long-tailed lizards
Who scramble through your branches daily
Then I left you behind for the cold, foggy crevices of
England

Coming home you waved your ever open arms
Welcoming this young heart whose merry laughter you'd
remembered
In distant land I thought of you

I remember how we used to play kick ball
Your aroma lingers and never goes
Been put in sweet, hot soup
I still love you
Even though you still grow in the backyard of my memory.

Iiola Ashundie

ZINDIKA KAMAUESI

I grew up in Jamaica and Britain. I was brought up by a
number of relatives and the community. Early movement in
my childhood I feel has given me the independent, travelling
and restless soul that I have.

I enjoy the writings of James Baldwin for his power and
passion and Toni Morrison for her beauty and craft - a
perfect combination to which I aspire
in my own writing.

Worlds Apart

There were four people in the photograph. Her grandfather pointed them out to her. One of them was her father dressed in a dark suit. He looked young, almost boyish in appearance. He was clean shaven with close-cropped hair and a smile that flattered his good looks. Alison had no memory of her father, but her grandfather spoke highly of him and sang his praises regularly.

"I raised him from a young boy to a man," he said proudly. "I'm glad he went to England."

"Why - was he a naughty boy?" Alison asked eagerly.

"Good Lord no! Of all the children I raised he was my favourite. I miss him."

"Why was he your favourite? What did he do?"

"He never forget me, no matter where he went." Alison sucked in her cheeks, a thousand questions on her mind. "And he left me his children to raise," her grandfather continued. "Not many people would do that." Alison listened intently, hanging onto every word her grandfather spoke about the man she did not know, but whose image lingered in her mind. "I just hope that him and you mother hurry up and send for you all soon, because I don't know what to do with girl children once they reach a certain age."

"Is England far?" Alison asked daydreaming of the place she had heard so much about and the family she hardly knew.

"Yes, far, far, but don't worry, you'll be going by plane - aeroplane. Up there." Her grandfather pointed to the sky.

"When?"

"Soon."

Yes, but how far was far and how soon was soon, Alison was thinking. Soon couldn't come soon enough for her. Talk of the impending journey had made her edgy and restless. She was tired of people asking her, when are you going to England? It was frustrating having to admit that she didn't know when. She felt as though there was a dark rain cloud hanging over her head and she could not bear the thought that any day now, sooner or later, she would be uprooted, torn from her grandfather, her friends and despatched to foreign parts like a parcel.

"You must do well at school and learn you lesson, so you can make you mother and father proud," her grandfather continued, not noticing her lack of excitement. "I don't want to send dem no dunce pickney."

Alison came top of the class every year in the annual school tests. Each year the test results were posted and pupils gathered around the notice board as if their fate was sealed by the number lying next to their name. The news always spread like wild fire throughout the school, of who had come top and bottom as those were the only important positions. There was no in-betweens, just the bright and the dunce, shame and elation, those going to England and those staying behind.

'Going to England' and coming top of the class had elevated her and her brothers and sister to a high status in the small Bathsheba community. They were on the same levels as those children who lived in town; whose parents were lawyers, doctors and policemen.

Her best friend was a dentist's daughter who lived in a big house on the hill overlooking the post office, the library and the market square. After going through the two large, iron gates that opened and closed automatically, there was a long driveway uphill to her friend's house, passed the walls that overhung with bougainvillea. There was always a car and a jeep parked in the driveway. There was always a garden boy hovering sheepishly, either sweeping up leaves or some kind of debris from the yard.

Once inside the house the family treated her like a celebrity. "Oh Alison I heard you came top in the test. Congratulations. You'll be going to England soon. Your parents are going to be so proud of you."

Sometimes she was allowed to go inside the dental surgery and her friend's father would demonstrate the implements for extracting teeth.

"Would you like to become a dentist one day, Alison?" he asked. She shrugged her shoulders.

"Why not? you're bright enough. Still it's not a job for the faint-hearted." She didn't know what he meant.

"I did my training in England," he continued. "England is the place to be - you're a lucky girl." She always left the house laden down with small tubes of Colgate toothpaste, sweet smelling dental plasticine into which she would make impressions of her teeth and purifying tablets that made the water red.

Alison walked the two miles from the market town, where her friend lived, to her house regularly. She lived in a two-roomed house with her grandfather, her two brothers and sister. The house had a verandah and was surrounded by lots of land but there was no electricity or running water. Her grandfather never referred to them as poor, despite their hand-to-mouth existence - the house was clean and homely. A registered letter came every month from England, if they were lucky. It was not enough to feed or cloth four hungry and growing children, but her grandfather never bemoaned this fact though for he knew that her parents were saving for their passage.

Every evening her grandfather sat out on the verandah and smoked his pipe in a pondering manner. Alison liked to watch him fill his pipe. First he dug out the old dust and ashes from the pipe, sticking a blade of grass down the handle to clear it, drawing air through it sharply. When he was satisfied he would cut up the dry tobacco on a slab of wood and stuffed the tobacco into the pipe with his rough fingernail, kneading it in gently. He always lit the pipe with a match struck on the side of the verandah, or if there was an open fire going he would pull out a stick of wood from the fire. He puffed and puffed until the pipe began to glow red. Then, slouching back against the wall of the verandah he pulled one leg of his khaki trousers up to his knee, cocked the other leg up and sat there blowing smoke into the air. Occasionally he released the pipe from his thin mouth, scratched his rough unshaven chin and spat into the air.

His brow always curled and his mouth extended into a long frown whenever he did not know where the next meal was coming from. He somehow always overcame the situation, through his own efforts and with God's good grace. God will provide, he always said.

Next morning when Alison woke up the table was full. There were hardo bread, bun, chicken legs, saltfish, yam, bananas, crackers, sugar, milo, molasses and condensed milk. She wondered how her grandfather always managed to perform such a marvellous feat of conjuring up something out of nothing. All her grandfather ever talked about was the fact that he had four bright children - scholarship material, and that one day they would be going to England.

"Alison put on your shoes," her grandfather shouted as she ran about the yard barefooted.

"I don't like shoes."

"You must always wear shoes, what if you father turned up from England unexpectedly, he would tink I not bringing you up right."

"Is my father coming home from England?" she asked excited.

"No. I said what if..." her grandfather replied.

What if. What if. Alison thought. What if her father came home; she had some many questions she wanted to ask him. Why did they stay away so long? Why couldn't they all live in Jamaica as a family? Her grandfather was strong, but he was an old man with four boisterous children in his care. What if. What if. What if she never went to England. What if she never saw her parents again.

"The other children don't wear shoes," she moaned reluctantly pulling on her shoes.

"You not like the other children, you going to England."

Before going to England there had been numerous visits to Kingston with her brothers and sister. Pictures were taken, vaccinations got, clothes bought, and official papers signed. Everything happened in fours. It was always the four of them that went to Kingston. The four of them that had passport pictures taken. The four of them that had new outfits made for the journey. The four of them were going to England. At the last minute her grandfather broke the news that it would only be two of them as their parents could not afford the air fares. She felt hurt. She felt led astray and built up only to be let down. She didn't cry. She couldn't. How could her parents consider such a thing? Alison looked at her young brother and sister. They seemed unconcerned. Were they the lucky ones - to be staying, or was she the lucky one - to be going?

"I'm sorry it has to be like this," her grandfather said helplessly. "If they can't send for you all - they better off coming back here."

In the picture her mother stood beside her father in a plain cut, sleeveless dress with a scooped neck. The picture was in black and white but she imagined the dress was either pink or cream. Her mother had long, black hair in a beehive style. Alison had vague memories of her mother, and one of them was of her washing her long, thick, black hair in a white basin. People always commented on her 'pretty coolie' hair; just like

her mother's, they used to say. Her mother stood beside her
father looking stern and serious, unsmiling compared to her
father's more open and generous face. In the picture was also
her chubby face, baby brother, with an unruly afro, and her
older sister whose name she could not remember.

"That's your sister, Josephine," Grandfather said. She tun
big woman. She did leave here with your mother. She was
only little then." Alison scrutinised the picture.

"What is she wearing?" Alison asked pointing to the picture.
Her sister was wearing a long, black cardigan way down to
the ground and loose trousers which looked like a skirt and a
frilly, floppy blouse. In the village people dressed lightly for the
sun. The long, black cardigan seemed grand and overdressed
but the outfit fascinated her. She had never seen anything like
it before.

"This must be how they dress in England," Grandfather
said. "Yes, look at Miss Josephine, you sister a pop style inna
England."

The picture stayed in Alison's mind. Years later when she
arrived in England, she expected everyone to be dressed like
that.

* * * * *

At the airport, her family stood waiting, the way they had stood
in the photograph. The first person she noticed was her father
for she had looked forward to greeting this unknown man whom
her grandfather had elevated to magnanimous proportions in
her head. He smiled coolly in a shy manner and placed a
gentle peck on cheek, but said very little. Then she saw her
mother - a more familiar face. Her mother grabbed her suddenly
wailing in a ritualistic manner and hugged her to her bosom
nearly suffocating her.

When Alison had thought of England she never imagined

places, faces, houses or the climate. She simply thought of her family. Now at last they were reunited. Even, the people in the arrival lounge smiled, taking pleasure in their reunion.

Her older brother talked incessantly on the journey home. There were bursts of laughter in the car as he spoke in broad patois. Alison could not bear it and decided to keep quiet for fear of sparking the same reaction. She wished he would shut up. The laughter resounded and ricocheted in a mocking manner. Who were these strange people, Alison thought? Why were they laughing? What was so amusing about her accent? Alison wished she was back in Kingston where there was colour and life and no one laughed at the way she spoke. She had only just arrived but already she missed her friends, her grandfather and the blackness of the people. She leaned again the back seat and started to drift away, then above all the laughter she heard someone shouting her name.

"Alison, what's my name?" It was not a voice she was accustomed to hearing.

Alison opened her eyes and thought for a moment. Where was she? Who was this stranger's voice? She must be dreaming. She looked out of the window but did not recognise the landscape. She expected to see palm trees, mango trees, wide, open blue skies, but instead all she saw were long stretches of concrete, intermittent greenery and an overcast sky. She realised that she was sitting in the back of her father's red Ford Cortina; squashed between her new sister and older brother who had a severe case of verbal diarrhoea. Her brother was now flaying his arms about in demonstration of some minor incident on the plane when she had accidentally knocked over the serving tray, spilling the convenience packed food onto the floor. So comical was his display that her new family kept asking for an action replay which he provided, relishing the attention.

"What's my name?" her mother repeated above the noise.

Alison smiled because she knew the answer, she had seen her mother's name written many times in that uncontrollable round loops on the envelopes from England.

"Norma Smith," she replied succinctly, afraid her accent might cause great uproar. Her mother gasped and turned around in a scolding manner which surprised her. The car erupted into another bout of laughter at her answer.

"No, my name is not Norma. How can you call me Norma? You must call me Mummy." Alison was confused. Her mother had not asked her what she should call her, she had precisely asked 'what's her name' and she had told her accurately. Anyway she was nearly eleven now and had never called anyone Mummy.

Home was a large terrace mansion made from red bricks with large bay windows. It rose five storeys high into the air. There were steps leading up to the opulent looking front door with brass knockers and steps leading down into the basement. There were five other families in the house. Her family occupied two rooms on the second landing. The room they slept in was cluttered. It was filled with large cardboard boxes, as if her parents were expecting to move any minute. In the corner was a big television with radio and a fold-away stereo set combined. In the room was also a bed settee in which all four children slept. Everything in England seemed to be shared. Shared bed, shared homes, shared kitchen, shared bathroom, shared gardens.

"Josephine tek you sister into the bedroom, to your wardrobe and show her where to put her things," her mother yelled from the kitchen.

Her sister made a face. Alison didn't understand why. Ever since their arrival Josephine had been making faces and keeping her distance. She took her reluctantly to another room and flung open the wardrobe door. It was packed full of clothes all

belonging to her sister. Alison gasped with envy. She watched
as Josephine took out each piece of clothing and threw it up
against herself.

"This is a hotpants," she said posing. "Everyone is wearing
them now."

"Why is it called a hotpants?"

"Because it's a pant and you wear it when it's hot."

"But it looks like shorts. We wear shorts back home."

"Well here we call it hotpants"

She took out a dress. "This is a Mary Quant dress. I got it
in Carnaby street."

"Where's Carnaby Street? Can I go there with you?"

"No. You're too young."

"But I want a dress like that."

"You've got to have lots of money." Everything in the
wardrobe seemed to be either black or brown or some kind of
dark, dull colour. Her sister explained the cost of each item
and threw them on the bed until the wardrobe was nearly empty.
From the bottom of the wardrobe, she took out long, leather
boots which zipped up to the knee and a long coat that went
down to her ankles.

"You have to wear this in the winter, because it gets very
cold." Alison picked up the coat off the bed and ran her hands
across its rough surface. She had never worn a coat in her
life. "...and you've got to wear gloves and a hat," Josephine
said pulling on some gloves and a woolly hat for her to see.
Alison told herself that she wasn't looking forward to winter .
Already, summer was so dull, what would winter be like?
Josephine started to put the clothes back in the wardrobe saying
there was hardly any room in there for her.

The suitcase Alison had brought from Jamaica was half
empty and mostly it contained food stuff for the family sent by
her grandfather. She only had two suits of clothes, one was a
short pinafore that came half way up her thighs exposing her

long, thin legs and a white, puffed-sleeve blouse which her grandfather had made for her to wear to England. In fact she need not have bought a suitcase at last, but her grandfather had said you can't go to England empty-handed.

Her mother came into the room carrying some hangers.

"I thought I told you to mek room in the wardrobe," she scolded.

"There's no room," Josephine yelled and stormed out of the room.

"I know you not use to sharing, but you have to start sharing now," her mother said sternly and took control of the situation. With one clean sweep she swept the clothes in the wardrobe to one corner. She thrust the hangers into Alison's hand and looked down at her. Alison looked back into the stern face which was mellowing a little.

"Don't worry, I'm going to take you out tomorrow and buy you some new clothes for winter and for school," her mother said.

Alison pressed her nose against the clothes in the wardrobe, they smelt different, they smelt like the way things that arrived in parcels smelt. It was a soapy, chocolate smell - a rather indistinguishable smell. Nothing smelt like this in Jamaica. England smelt differently to Jamaica.

Life in England was miserable. The sunshine was gone. Alison found herself saying Mummy and Daddy quicker than she expected - but at the same time she felt herself descending into a deep, dark gloom.

The gloom expanded and crept up on her when she least expected it. One afternoon as she played out on the pavement in the late summer sunshine with Josephine - the neighbour who lived in the basement of their house, came up the steps adjusting her raincoat over her nurse's uniform. She saw them playing gaily together and smiled.

"Josephine, aren't you lucky you have brothers and sisters

to play with now? I've never seen you look so happy,she remarked. Josephine stopped skipping suddenly.

"I'm not playing with her and she's not my sister" Josephine yelled in a high pitch voice and stormed off. The skipping rope handle clattered to the pavement and Alison remained motionless for a while before she could pick it up. Alison's biggest fear was that one day her sister would deny her and now it had happened. Why did Josephine not like her, she asked herself?

"Never mind, Alison," the neighbour remarked. "She not use to sharing. She's had her mummy and daddy to herself all these years. What a selfish girl." Alison picked up the skipping rope and continued to skip on her own. She skipped until her legs grew tired, then she folded the skipping rope into a ball and went indoors. She threw the rope into a corner and slumped onto the settee smarting with anger.

Alison knew it was only in her imagination - but she always felt that her mother and father loved her sister, more than they loved her. Often, when her mother was annoyed with her she would shout, why can't you be more like Josephine. Josephine was bright, outgoing and she had lots of friends. Josephine had been in England a long time and had developed English ways. There was a picture of her on the wall, she looked studious and academic, dressed in her school uniform with her satchel in her left hand. There was also a picture of Alison's mother and father and her baby brother on the wall. Alison wondered when her picture would go onto the wall with all the other family portraits but it never did. She only ever took one picture with the family, once when it was her baby brother's birthday and then she was on the edge and the photographer had cut her face in half; and that was how she always felt, half, never whole. Whereas Josephine's face stood out beaming in the middle of the photograph as if it was her birthday. Alison felt guilty for thinking certain thoughts - ungrateful thoughts her

mother might say, after all she had worked hard, and sent for
her and her brother to come to England. But, if only, her mother
would put her picture on the wall, that would make everything
allright.

That night, Alison dreamt of Jamaica. She was in Kingston.
She was sitting out on the verandah in the hot sun. It melted
every crevice of her body and filled her with warmth and
happiness. All around her, the doors to the houses were flung
open and cooking smells mingled with the perfumed buds falling
from the pungent fruit laden trees. The children living next
door shouted out her name across the garden fence, the
hawkers rode by on bicycles selling their wares, shouting
'peanuts!' "Alison, Alison," the children called, and she raced
out into the yard to play hopscotch and marbles. Then she
woke up and her sister was sitting beside her in bed - calling
her to wake up, and complaining that she had been talking in
her sleep. Alison wondered how two people could be so close
and yet be so far apart. She looked around the room. Unusually,
she noticed that the television was on, but showing a fuzzy
picture. Then she remembered her dream. It was so real. It
had refreshed her. The television crackled and died. Her sister
jumped off the bed and banged it back into life. One of the
things she missed about Kingston was being able to watch
American television which she liked very much. In England,
the television was rarely on because her father had banned
them from watching too much television, preferring them to
study their books. He made it clear that they had come to
England to get a good education because there was little else
to be got.

Winter came and there was snow on the ground. Alison
ran out into the garden to taste the snow. It melted swiftly.
She made snowballs and chased her brother. The changing
seasons was something she enjoyed, because everything was
fresh and hopeful and at last she had something to write home

about. Like the seasons, she and her sister were changing, not in harmony but further apart.

Her sister was getting fat. Everyone commented on how fat she was getting. She became size conscious - checking her weight continuously. Alison was pleased. At least she was not fat. She prayed for her sister to get fatter and fatter but her sister went on a diet. She screeched everytime her mother put something threatening fat on her plate. She ate, salad, nimble and Ryvita. Nimble tasted like yeuch and ryvita was like cardboard, except it became mildly palatable when it had lashings of Blueband margarine on it. The only thing Alison liked about nimble was the girl floating off in the balloon. *She flies like a bird in the skyyyy. She flies like a bird...oh me oh my....I see her fly.* Alison wished she could fly away from England and be free.

In the ryvita advert when the woman turns to face the camera her waist becomes a tape measure. Her waist was twenty two inches. Alison had a twenty six inch waist and she became mildly horrified everytime she looked down at her stomach. She told her mother that she wanted to go on a diet and her mother laughed out loud.

"Diet my foot, you maaga like. You too damn follow fashin. Follow fashin monkey bruk him back."

A letter arrived from Jamaica - a begging letter according to her mother. Her mother threw down the letter on the table and Alison picked it up. It was the usual letter from her grandfather, much like the ones she had written herself, but now she was in England.

"You grandfather always want money," her mother nagged. "Him tink money grow pon tree over here. Him tink we living rich inna England. Is no last month me send him money." Alison wanted to shout at her mother, telling her the money was not enough, but the hurt inside was too much. Her mother wouldn't listen. Her mother never listened. Her mother would not really understand. It seemed that she was the only one who understood. It was like being caught between two worlds. People in Jamaica didn't know what life was really like in England and people in England had forgotten what life was like in Jamaica.

   She could see the two worlds, torn apart - out of sight out of mind. She wished her mother and father would hurry up and send for her brother and sister - but now their marriage was on the rocky road to ruin the possibility of seeing her younger brother and sister was remote.

                                              Zindika Kamauesi

Putting Down Roots

Five years became fifty years and before long we were
saying 'We are here to stay'. The cold British winters
were survived with some sturdy clothes huddled in front
of our paraffin heaters. In spite of the difficulties children
adjusted to their new family, they were, after all, our own
flesh and blood.

The biggest challenge faced was in adjusting to the
outside world. Tentatively we ventured out from our big
communal houses - only to find that the people were
just as cold as the climate.

For many, their first experience of the wider society
was at school where they became the only black face -
an object of curiosity. Maxine Raymond recalls "I made
friends very quickly becoming a source of fascination
for some...not many had contact with other black people."

We might have been here to stay but we were not
necessarily wanted or welcomed. We noticed we were
in the minority, colourwise, and for the first time learnt
that we were black and discovered prejudice in many
forms. Both Maxine Raymond and Muditasri remember
being the victims of name calling. It was at school that
they first heard words like 'wog', 'nigger', and 'jungle
bunny'. At school they first learnt what racism was. "I
always gave the impression that I had not heard, but I
smarted with pain and anger." We watched our parents
how they gritted their teeth and got on with it. We soon
learnt to say that 'sticks and stones may break my bone
but words cannot hurt me.'

Education was to be our meal ticket. Our parents had
told us so. The rigours of the Caribbean education

system meant that most of the children who came here were well-educated but soon became miseducated, demoted and kept back under the streaming system which existed at the time.

Children had to watch their parents go through the colour bar society in housing and jobs. Many rooms were advertised as 'No blacks, Irish or dogs', but as Muditasri points out they also went onto say 'no children'. In her piece *'A Different Climate'* she recalls the itinerant and embarrassing lifestyle her family led as they were unable to find permanent accommodation. "Between the ages of 11 and 19 when I left home, our family had moved seventeen times. It caused me many moments of acute embarrassment and fear, traces of which are still in me today."

Many parents still tried to hang on to their old traditions and values from back home in the food, the music, the accent and their strict child-rearing. However, the children who came were young enough to be adaptable. Being in England meant putting the Caribbean behind in order to fit in and get on. We quickly acclimatised. Soon we got to liking pie and chips and baked beans. We started to turn our nose up at yam and banana, ackee and saltfish. That was the food our parents ate. We tried to straddle two cultures for a while but as we became accustomed to the British way of life - one inevitably overshadowed the other.

From their two-roomed beginnings most parents saved and tried to buy themselves a little piece of England. Back home the children were used to seeing white people from afar in their cars and from behind the high perimeter walls of their homes - now we were living next door to white people, they were our friends.

Declan Joseph in *'The Unsung Journey'* states, "By

the 1980s the English way of life has been so widely
adopted by us, that all sense of values that we came with
and should have retained have now been - if not lost,
virtually owned by others."

The young migrants who came over were now
unrecognisably British and westernised. They became
the face of the new Black Britain.

MAXINE RAYMOND

I emigrated to Britain from the Caribbean (St. Vincent) in 1975 at the age of 9. The grey, dismal sky and foreboding atmosphere that greeted me at Heathrow Airport that bitterly cold February morning in '75 were perhaps indicative of how drastically my life would change.

Over the years I have developed an understanding of how the intense and traumatic effect of being a child emigré impacted on me. I have accepted that I cannot change the past, but I have some input in my future.

I am a keen writer and I think just by sharing my experiences I am doing something positive.

Miss Raymond Queen

I had not wanted to come to England. Certainly, I did not want to leave behind Mummy and my extended family, nor indeed my friends. Yet, here I was waiting for Mother, dressed in ultra-trendy woollen, hipster trouser-suit, with its interwoven threads of blue, brown and white which Mummy had lovingly made. I should explain that 'Mummy' was actually my aunt - an older sister of my mother - she being the youngest daughter of my grandmother.

Mother and I had met, for the first time a few months earlier. Like many young men and women from the Caribbean, she left St. Vincent in order to develop her career and earn money to support her family. I was a baby when she left and therefore had no recollection of her while growing up. I recalled the fascination and pride I had for her on our first encounter. She was very slim, beautiful, ebony-complexioned and always seemed to begin or finish every sentence with the exclamation 'honestly', and of course she was my very own mother.

In terms of looks I had taken nothing from my mother. My light brown complexion and wavy hair resembled my father, with whom, incidentally, I had no contact, except for seeing him across the river imploring me to come to him, then me running away. On one such occasion tripping over a bolder, which subsequently saw the big toenail of my right foot totally ripped away. To this day, I remember the shooting pain caused by the iodine used to soothe - and I use that word sparingly - my sore toe.

Nowadays Father would probably be referred to as an absent father. He migrated to Canada in 1972. I was not to see or hear from him again until 1990. As a girl I aspired to live as a family with both my mother and father. Indeed, I visualised the scenario often. It never was to be and would remain forever a dream. His absence from my life had a profound effect on me and I believe, contributed greatly to the person I became.

It might be construed quite wrongly that I did not want to be with mother. I did, but preferably in St.Vincent. England was vast, imposing and impersonal. This was completely alien to what I had previously known. In the Northern town that was to become my home for ten years, every house looked the same; a mass of brown bricks. I missed the brightly coloured houses of my birthplace, as well as the rivers, the sea, the food and my family and friends. The people however did seem friendly. They said hello and made me feel welcomed - up North. I thought this was how it would always be. The television too helped to endear me to England and I became avidly addicted to it. 'Hong Kong Phooey' and 'Crossroads' immediately spring to mind.

The relationship between Mother and me did not turn out the way I expected. We appeared to have absolutely nothing in common - the maternal bonding was lacking. She was expecting a baby when I arrived in England and soon afterwards married the father of her impending child - a widower, originally from Jamaica. Subsequently we moved in with him and his children. I could not come to terms with this relationship, particularly the violence that occurred within. I wanted to help Mother, but as a nine year old child there was nothing I could do. I had never witnessed abuse before. All I could do was try to ensure that my attitude reflected the resentment I felt towards him. Years later, I was told by a disgruntled relative that I was the cause of the break-up of my mother's marriage.

The violent scenes I witnessed made it difficult for me to

relate to mother. I could not speak to her, even today, I am not sure why. The lack of dialogue and closeness persisted for many years. Perhaps, looking back I wanted Mother to myself. After all I did not have her for those important early stages of my childhood. To come from a place filled with an abundance of love where I was made to feel the centre of attention made it difficult for me to acclimatise to the different way of life I was leading in England. I suppose you could say I was spoilt. Certainly my long hair and skin tone meant I was put into the category of those with 'good hair' and 'pretty skin'. My family even dubbed me 'Miss Raymond Queen'. Later I would realise that this classification was little more than a subtle divide and rule tactic perpetuated by the former colonialists, as a means of keeping black people in their place since slavery days.

However, I believe that the more intense reason for being treated so very special and given so much attention by my extended family was because of the absence of my biological mother. Additionally, I was a child who suffered much ill-health, the most serious being rheumatic fever, which culminated in my developing a heart defect. The needle phobia that I suffer today directly stems from numerous penicillin injections I was prescribed as a child.

The seeming demotion in my status, affected me greatly and the strained relationship between Mother and her husband added to this. Much of the love I had known and taken for granted in St.Vincent had on the face of it disappeared. Mother did love me. I know this now, she just didn't know how to show it. She was then and remains today a shy person. She was young and had tried her best to get somewhere in the world. Life just dealt her an unlucky hand. It happened that there were others with whom she had to share her love.

Primary school was an eye-opener. It was multi-ethnic and as such I found it easy to adapt, albeit that I thought my Vincentian accent sounded terrible and made a conscious effort not to speak too much for about three months, until I had mastered the English twang. Now I regret my determination to lose my accent. It was at this school that I was first introduced to the words 'nigger' 'wog' and 'jungle bunny' and here that I came to the realisation that I was a black person and as such, different from the indigenous population - a second-class citizen.

Both girls and boys wore their hair in afros, which was the style at the time. I found this bizarre. Little girls in St.Vincent wore their hair braided and decorated with beautiful ribbons and boys' hair was always neatly cut. Uniform was also part and parcel of this and worn with pride. The pupils here did not appear to have any pride in their uniform.

I found the educational system very different. There was still the encouragement to gain top grades albeit less emphasised, but there was also less discipline as children swore in class, and were generally very disruptive. Having been brought up to fear God, it was instilled in me from an early age that I must not swear. The only word I would say was 'damn' and my excuse was that it was in the Bible. I had read a children's book which told the story of a little girl who lied and swore. It so happened that each time she did either, a black ant would bite away at her heart and they would continue to congregate there as long as she persevered in her bad ways. This terrified me. I wanted God to love me, and most of all, I didn't want black ants to devour my heart.

I was always top of the class in St. Vincent. Competitions to achieve the best results were encouraged and prizes were given to the top three pupils. I remember one term coming second and bursting into tears. I worked harder thereafter to ensure that this never happened again. In England, I began to change.

Mixing with other black children, I soon learned of the inter-island differences that existed. The children of Jamaican parentage, who were the majority, adopted their own form of Jamaican patois, which they would use to great effect, in portraying how cool or hard they were. Those whose parents were from other islands would pretend to be Jamaican. I used to think they were very silly. I was from the Caribbean, trying to erase my accent and here they were trying to gain one. Surely they were confused!

Subsequently, I would be targeted as 'a small island monkey eater' and such other colloquialisms, by my English-Jamaican peers.

When Mother eventually left her abusive relationship, I was forced to change schools. This time I became the only black child. There was however, a marked difference in this school. There was pride in wearing the uniform and the Headmaster was very strict. I made friends quickly, becoming a source of fascination for some. I learnt there that I was different from other black people and 'allright for a black girl'. Not that many of them had contact with other black people. I also learnt to say the dreaded 'F' word. I still feared God, but began to believe that the Ladybird book was wrong, or at the very least, over-dramatic. My interest in learning waned somewhat and I joined in with a bunch of rebellious kids, becoming quite troublesome, though funny with it. I didn't fight. I was simply naughty. I also had a quaint ability to make people laugh and I believe that this helped in my being accepted. Gone forever was the me of old.

I recalled an Asian teacher came to the school. Known for her strictness, everyone feared her. She was never afraid to mete out punishment to any child. She said something very profound to me, that I dismissed at the time. She told me that as a black person I would have to work twice as hard to achieve anything in this country, but hey, I was a rebel and I didn't care. Anyway, adulthood was a long way away.

I was by contrast a quiet withdrawn child at home. Mother

worked nights and this brought its own problems. At ten I was no longer a child. This was reinforced all the more one day after feeling I was surely dying having bled for three days. I confided in Mother and learned that I would have to suffer the humiliating indignity monthly for many years. I was told not to let boys touch me and given a book on the facts of life to read. I was scared, but there was nothing I could do. What was to become of me?

My body developed quickly thereafter. I was a child trapped in a woman's body which brought another set of issues. Mother continued to shower most of her love on my baby sister. I wondered whether she cared about me at all. I certainly did not think so and nothing she did appeared to suggest the reverse. My sister was the only one of mother's children whom she would nurture from birth and, perhaps in her own way, she was learning to be a parent. This did not help me then. I felt isolated, wholly alone. I yearned for the comfort of Mummy, I yearned for someone who would care about me. I cried out for love, but no one came to give that love to me. I protected Mother from my feelings because I did not want to cause her distress. Because of this, it never crossed my mind to inform those back in St. Vincent of my plight. I had stopped writing to them. Years later I found a book in which I had written 10 wishes. One was that I would be taken into care, another that Mother and my sister would always be happy, and another that I would go to live with my father.

It is now as an adult, I realise how difficult things were for Mother. She had little support and she too was learning. However, at that time, as a little girl, from a close extended family living on a small idyllic island, my coming to a country that, by comparison seemed cold and unfeeling, was painful in the extreme. Those early years in England, is a period of my life that remain painful to recollect, even though later events were fraught with much more misery.

I often wonder how things would have been, had I stayed in St.Vincent. I believe that on that tiny island there was a strong sense of belonging, that incorporated the wider community. For me unfortunately childhood emigration had a detrimental effect. I, however, learned many things, which makes me the person I am today. I have learned to be sensitive, non-judgemental and after many years, to love and believe in myself.

The other day I came to the realisation that I have lived over two-thirds of my life in England. I have reached a point where I cannot imagine living anywhere else. Apart from my addiction to soaps and imported US talk shows - a constant source of annoyance to friends, I sincerely feel that the opportunity to achieve at least some of the goals I have is here. I believe I owe it to myself to grasp the opportunities I have.

It has been a long time and a difficult struggle to arrive at this point. I have had to learn to believe in myself, to maintain my integrity and have control over my own life. As a part of this process, I have developed an understanding of how intense and traumatic the effect of being a child emigre impacted on me. I have accepted that I cannot change the past, but I can have my input in the future. Just sharing this short episode of my life between the ages of 9 and 12, I feel I am doing something positive. My hope is that it gives an insight into my experience and therefore promotes understanding of me.

Maxine Raymond

EUREKA HUNTE

I have been writing since the age of ten. As a black woman who is a professional trainer, social worker, writer and, most importantly, a mother of four and now a grandmother, I feel that writing, performing and storytelling are all part of the learning, giving, sharing, living and healing processes of life. Where there's life, there's hope. I give thanks to the creator and my ancestors who have guided me thus far.

From Paraffin to Central Heating Days

Experiences of migration have been tough on us black folks, not just physically but mentally, emotionally and spiritually. My experiences, though not as traumatic as some, have left me feeling disenfranchised in a country which should by rights be my home. But home is where the heart is and my heart and my spirit are definitely not here in South London. I still feel like a foreigner or an alien, a term psychologists prefer to use.

My entry into this country was May 1957. I arrived from Barbados with my mother and my brother on a spring day. My mother has told me that the journey on the ship was one of the worst experiences of her life. She was seasick and found it difficult to keep nursing me as I was a baby. Fortunately for her, she met another woman, also from Barbados, who helped her with both myself and my brother Noel. My father was already up here orchestrating a five-year plan and working as a conductor and driver on the buses with London Transport.

Life as we knew it started with rented rooms, some of these I remember sharing with other migrants, racist abuse from white people, harassment from Jamaican migrants, poverty and neglect from nannies. Progressive racism and prejudice compounded many of my family's problems.

An experience which stands out prominently in my mind, like it was yesterday, were the winter days and the fog filled atmosphere. It wasn't just the physical cold but the psychological struggle of surviving the cold. As a child I suffered from chilblains and I still do. I used to get them on my toes and feet. Now they were all over my legs from top to toe and guess where else, yes you guessed it, my bum! So you see, even my physical body has been traumatised by the cold!

Typically, in the Caribbean household, I could guarantee that I, along with many others, were taking cod liver oil, malt syrup and castor oil. Aak! Not to mention the occasional Epsom salts. Plus there was Pap, what is commonly known as Scottish Porridge oats. I am sure that if it wasn't for our parents feeding us with those remedies and insulating foods, we would have surely perished.

Anyway, as a child, it was up to my brother and I to go out like hunters and gatherers to bring back the fuel for the fire and heat. The fuel being paraffin. There we were, both on foot, no more that four feet tall each, carrying metal and plastic gallon cans. My brother, who was the eldest, would be carrying three cans and I would be carrying two.

In those days, it was pink paraffin that was used, in the early '70s, blue paraffin was introduced which smelt equally nasty as the pink. There was no age restriction laws then as to who could buy paraffin, not like those placed on petrol today.

Friday evenings were the days we would go and fetch the paraffin. My brother and I would come home from school, have something to eat and get to grips with our chores. Sometimes we would get the paraffin after our parents returned home from work or, on the occasions when we went before they arrived from work, there would be a note on the table written by our mother saying, "Get four or five gallons of paraffin. See what the money could bring. Love mummy."

Reading the note was the easy part, carrying the cans was another thing! My brother and I would gather the cans, putting some in a carrier bag and make our way down to the hardware store.

My brother was what I would call a lingerer. He would loiter, kick everything in his path, (yer see he loved football), day-dream and of course we would skylark and chase each other, as children do. Fetching the paraffin was our time, our special time. There were no adults telling us what to do or where to walk. No adult telling me to walk properly or wringing my ear. No adults saying "Wait till you get home". We would talk about everything from our parents and the way they used to beat us for fighting at school. We even used to quarrel on the street, but despite that, I truly loved my brother. He was like my protector and still is to a certain extent.

The fun only lasted as long as the cans were empty. Once the cans were filled our physical struggles began. Our hands would be sore and blistered. Our arms would ache. To me, it felt like torture, sheer torture. My brother and I would stop every now and then to shift the can from one arm to another, believing that this would help. I would lick the callus on the palm of my hands to keep them moist. I felt sorry for my brother more than myself, because he was carrying three cans and I was only carrying two. Nevertheless we were both struggling.

There were occasions when my brother and I would have to go further afield to get the paraffin especially if the store had sold out. This is where our physical struggle was compounded by fear. Pangs of pain would start welling up inside me because I knew my parents, especially my father would not believe that we had to go to another shop. My brother was always quite cool. He always tried to reassure me by saying, "Don't worry Lorr. He ain't gonna beat us." When we got in Daddy would be there waiting like a cat for a mouse. The first thing he would ask us was "Where unno go?" Our reply was always the same ."Nowhere Daddy. We had to go to another shop." Sometimes no matter what we said or how we said it, it always sounded like a lie. Do I have to tell you what followed? You guessed it - the lashes. Big heavy-handed lashes. Lashes you will never forget.

As a child I was always reminded all too often of what my

parents had to do before they went to school. My parents would say, "Before we left for school back home we had to fetch water from the standpipe, then we had to wet the kitchen garden, or we had to milk the cow." Didn't they realise they bought us to this country where there were no standpipes, no cows to milk? So whose fault was it? Surely not ours. There was nothing we could do which would compare or assimilate to their struggle. For me, carrying a gallon of paraffin was somehow symbolically similar to my parents gallon of water from the standpipe.

Our parents thought that we had it easy in comparison to them and in some ways we did. But our struggles were our struggles and their struggles were our struggles too! So you see, carrying paraffin was not just a necessity for our household, or about giving us responsibilities; it was also attached to cultural traditions which were somehow recreated in the hope that we would feel empathy with their experiences. Now times have changed and we have moved from paraffin, to gas central-heating days.

Eureka Hunte

JANET CARON

I have lived in Britain since 1957. I have little or no knowledge of my country of birth. This book has enabled me to tap into my memory and rediscover my childhood since arriving in Britain.

From an early age I enjoyed making things. My choice of material has gone from making pies in the back yard in Guyana to oil painting on ceramics. I have had various exhibitions in London.

In 1994, I joined 'Word for Word' a Haringey based writers' group. Weekly creative writing sessions gave me the opportunity to read and get feedback on my work. I have also contributed to 'Scribes and Passion' and a number of other anthologies and magazines. This has given me the confidence to continue writing and reading my work. I have a number of projects in the planning and research stage.

The Old Schoolyard

I t was a cold Monday morning in April 1958 at Chankwell Junior School in the East End of London. The sun was shining weakly in a grey-blue sky. Children were buzzing around the school yard, the sound of their voices escaping over the roof-top. The ringing of the bell summoned us inside the red brick building two by two. We scurried swiftly through the corridor to the cloakroom to hang up our coats.

In our classroom there was the dependable Miss Roberts already behind her dark wooden desk, chivvying us along with only a look from her stern, blue eyes, made larger by thick glasses which gave her the appearance of an owl. I laughed. She smiled back not knowing my private joke.

"Come along children, settle down. Quiet."

Instant silence.

"Now before we start our lesson I want to introduce you all to Paulo Vincenti, he is going to be in our class."

We all stared at the boy. He was thin and the tiny white shorts he had on made his legs look like a couple of bean poles. He looked worried. I could see it in his large brown eyes as his gaze flicked around the classroom. I felt a little sorry for him. I knew what it was like to be new and out of place. It was only a couple of years ago that I had been the new one. I had been stared at and wondered about, until I made friends in the playground.

I was very shy, and the behaviour of the children made me conscious of being an outsider. One day I saw them playing a skipping game and I hung about until one of the girls eventually asked me to join them. Over a few terms of being in the

class, a kind of acceptance was gained along with the ability
to blend in. My face wasn't new anymore and I no longer
stuck out as different.

I really liked Paulo and would have liked to have befriended
him but a friendship developed between him and another brown-
skinned girl. Her plaits were done up all neatly with pretty,
blue ribbons. They were inseparable, even with taunts, finger
pointing and the giggles from the rest of the class, they didn't
seem to care. I remember at a singing lesson , the piano was
being played in the corner by the teacher. We were learning
Greensleeves. I was really singing loud, trying to impress the
teacher. I turned to see Paulo and his friend with their two
heads together as he whispered in her ear, totally oblivious of
the rest of the class. I felt the sharp stab of jealousy and found
myself wishing that I too had a friend to tell me stories that
would make me forget my surroundings. I lost interest in singing
and then just mimed the words to the song. My mouth opened
and closed like a goldfish in a small, round bowl.

I didn't tell Mum about my feelings for Paulo. I didn't
think she would understand and she might have thought it
strange or wrong that I had a crush on a boy at my age. Back
in Guyana such feelings weren't heard of in nine-year-olds.
Back home childhood lasted longer. Even when I was thirteen
years old, under the Christmas tree, the presents were always
two dolls, one for me and one for my sister.

Mum and Dad had not been to school in this country, so
they had no experience of school life to pass on to us. Also
they were probably too busy learning about the ways of life in
their new country. From the simplest lesson, like whether to
put the milk in first when pouring a proper cup of English tea -
to the more extreme lessons of toughening themselves against
the name calling of 'Blackie go home' or how to rent a flat or
rooms. They often turned up to view accommodation in their
best clothes and eager smiles, but they were always met with

sullen face landladies. They had come to Britain full of optimism regarding the opportunities that we would find for a new life. Dad was a printer by trade and didn't have too much trouble finding work as a printer in the city. To make ends meet Mum had to work and so she didn't have time to meet me and my sister after school like other mums.

After school we went to the home of Maureen and her brother Jack. Maureen had dead straight hair cut into a bob and held in place with a pink hair slide. Jack had thick, mouse-coloured hair made tidy by a visit to the barbers, but at the back of his head he had a 'Dennis the Menace' bit of hair that refused to lie down. He didn't appear to notice or care about his hair. He kept white mice, which often escaped into his room and under the bed and Jack was forever looking for one of his mice.

Their family lived in a block of flats which was ten storeys high. I was a little afraid to stand on the small balcony, even when the others said, "Look your mum is coming", I hung back thinking that that small oblong piece of concrete did not look too safe.

After school each day we would bustle into Jack and Maureen's flat, Maureen calling out, "Mum we're back, anything to eat?" There was always something to eat. Everyday their mother made fish-paste sandwiches cut into small, white triangles, and a small, green apple tart. If it rained we ate in the flat, or off a cloth spread out on the carpet for a pretend picnic, while their mum and a woman friend sat in the kitchen, chatting, smoking and drinking endless cups of tea. The best time was when the weather was dry. We took our food and ate in a nearby park. There was a secret glade, surrounded by trees on a slide where we played hide and seek 'til Mum came to collect us.

Me and my younger sister had travelled from Guyana in 1957 to be reunited with Mum and Dad in this cold, grey land of Britain. I missed the tropical sun and Mama's (Granny's) garden with its mango, banana, soursop and star apple trees. Those fruits could not be found in the shops in England, so feeling sorry for us, our granny sent us food parcels with the essentials like Cassrip, tins of butter, and tangy tamarind paste.

Our first home in England was a rabbit warren of a house that made lots of money for the landlords as every room that could be rented was rented out. We had two rooms on the first floor. The larger one was where we lived. There was a large bed for Mum and Dad and some chairs and a black and white television with a tiny, white screen in a large, wooden cabinet. Lots of photographs on the display cupboard with a glass door where Mum kept her precious glasses, some brought safely all the way from Guyana. Lacy, crocheted doilies were laid on every possibly surface in the room.

My sister and I slept on beds in the other room which was also the kitchen. There was not much in the way of furniture but we didn't care as we made our own fun. My favourite toy were soldiers lined up in ranks on a chair, with movement created by shaking the chair. It was my sister who requested this present and we spent lots of happy hours with those plastic toy soldiers.

At weekends there was always a party somewhere to cheer us up. A party with friends from the old country, where the adults ate, drank and talked noisily in smoke filled rooms. There was always lots of beautiful food. Food was an important part of West Indian parties. We kids liked watching the mums as they brought lots of food to put out on the table. We waited until we were told we could start. Then we piled into rice and peas, cold chicken salad, spice beef curry, special meat and veg patties that the mums made. Then came desert: rich, black fruit cake, moist with rum and whisky, light golden sponges, fruit salad, ice cream and glasses of home-made gingerbeer so strong it felt as if your throat was on fire. We stuffed ourselves 'til we thought we would burst. After an hour or so of running around and dancing we were back to the table for more. I remember being urged to try something new - Souse, creepy - a soft, pink meat of pigs feet and tail with garlic and limes sitting in a transparent jelly, with slices of cucumber dotted here and there in a large metal bowl. It was strange to look at but it tasted better than it looked.

When it got late, the calypso or blue beat music was replaced with Nat King Cole or Jim Reeves records and all the kids were herded into a room with mattresses and blankets and told to go to sleep. Impossible. Instead we told each other silly jokes.

"What do you get if you cross a collie dog and a jelly?" Answer: "the collie wobbles." And always the tongue twisters, repeating "Red lorry, yellow lorry" fast to see if it made sense. The hardest one was, "She sells sea shells by the sea shore..." interrupted by someone moaning, "Ahh, you pig"

"What, it wasn't me!" Nobody wanted to own up to passing wind. Eventually we would fall asleep to be woken when it was light and the adults were ready to go home.

At the end of summer in 1960 we moved to North London with its quiet, tree-lined streets. The move was distracting and stopped me thinking too much about Paulo. The move was carried out in secret. Why, I was never sure. Dad just said, "Don't tell anyone we're moving." There was no question of our obedience to Dad. Besides it pleased me to be part of a family conspiracy. It made me feel like a secret agent. The excitement of moving kept the worry down of what would happen to the family if I spilt the beans. Would the baddies come around and stop us leaving? Would it involve guns and knives? Paulo faded from my mind for a while, returning a few weeks after we settled into the new house.

It was all ours and Dad got the chance to play landlord and chose who could rent a room on top of the two floors of our house. I was in the dining room with Dad and his boyhood friend Pipey. His nickname suited him well, because he always smelt of whiskey and tobacco smoke. They had come to England together. I had seen the black and white photographs in the album. There is one of a group of about twelve men posing on the steps of a house. They all looked like something out of an old movie, with their zoot suits and Bogart hats pulled down over their eyes. They had all come over to Britain to work and get homes before sending for their families. I wondered if Dad had been lonely waiting a whole year 'til Mum arrived and then another year for me and my sister to come to our new life in the 'mother country', as Dad liked to call Britain.

Pipey was a regular visitor to our house. If there was a party he would be there with one of 'pipey's women' as Mum called them. He would always encourage the kids to dance or tell their timetables.

"You have grown into a big girl. Have you got a boyfriend?" Pipey enquired with a inquisitive smile. Then I remembered Paulo and replied indignantly with a little sad smile, "Yes he is a boy and he's my friend." Even though Pipey insisted, I would not tell him the name of my friend. I never told anyone about Paulo until now.

                                                        Janet Caron

A Bottle Full of Memories

A big belly, black man
Clean white shirt buttoned up to
reveal brown skin dotted with
tight black chest curls
leading up to a round small face

Bright, dark eyes
look out from behind
his happy face masked
Does he let it drop
after exchanging greetings

What memories of home
haunt his nights
Make him wake in fright
To a cold window pane
dripping English rain
and reach for the bottle of rum

Drink, drink down the memory
of the sun-warmed sea wall beneath him
Blue, the piercing sky
Squinting up to catch
sight of the orange kite
flying high, flying free

Drink, drink down the memory
of rain water running
from finger-tips to elbow
leaning out the window anything
to grasp the Ginnep an' hold tight
cracking the skin to

sweet tart numbness on the tongue
A mouthful of taste for such a small fruit

Drink, drink down the memory
the sight of aunty, uncle and granny
waving from the shores
The green land floating far far away
The distant roars of breakers
echoing in the head and in the heart

Drink, drink down the memory
a bottle full of memories.

Janet Caron

MUDITASRI

Muditasri came to Birmingham, England with her mother
at the age of eleven. On leaving school she worked as a
secretary, telegraphist and had various office jobs. She
moved to London at the age of nineteen. The following
years saw her hitch-hiking through Western Europe
out of sheer curiosity and her love of the Spanish
language. That experience laid the foundation for
her love of travel which has taken her as far
afield as Asia, Australia and New Zealand.

She qualified as a social worker in 1976 at a time when
black social workers were rare. She has worked
in many areas of social work and in the late 1980s to
the mid-'90s worked as a trainer of social workers
and those in allied professions.

She has been a Buddhist for twenty years and in 1989
was ordained into the Western Buddhist Order. She
now spends her time teaching meditation and Buddhism
and engaging in various writing projects, one of
which is her autobiography.

A Different Climate

W e were fairly well off by Caribbean standards. We owned a four-roomed house with kitchen. My father was in full employment and my mother worked within the home caring for us. By the age of six however, our fortunes had changed. My father died suddenly and my mother was left with the responsibility of raising three children.

On the island of St. Kitts there was very little work for women - with the exception of house servants in the homes of the rich, white colonials who seemed not to realise that slavery had been abolished. My mother's own aspirations had been thwarted by lack of parental support and having to care for her younger siblings. She did not want the same for us. However, in order to provide the basic necessities she was forced to work long, unsocial hours which meant spending less time with us, 'her three jewels'. Through necessity, from the age of eight, I took over some parenting tasks. My mother was giving some consideration to seeking a new life in England. She had even acquired a passport which remained unused for some time. However, one event triggered the final decision to leave.

I was always a light sleeper and could never fully settle until mother returned from her work in the restaurant. As usual on her return we exchanged news. On this particular night the news was not good. I related that my two siblings had been reluctant when called to terminate their play and in an attempt to hasten them indoors I had chased them and, losing my shoes had been badly cut by a piece of glass. As I write I can, once again hear my mother's words: "I live on the same island as my children and cannot put them to bed, don't see enough of them, that being the case I shall go to England and work for you all and start a new life". I was then ten years old.

Within days my mother had renewed her passport and the wheels were set in motion. Would she really leave St.Kitts and go to England this time? Against all advice she decided to bring me with her believing I was too close to maturity to be left behind. A few months later we were on our way to England, my two siblings being left behind in the care of her eldest brother.

Three weeks on the ocean is a long time especially as my only acquaintance with the sea had been a tentative paddle as near to the shore as possible. However, in the June of 1960 we staggered off the train at Paddington station and were met by my mother's youngest brother who had been living in England for about seven years. He had not only come to meet us but more importantly to him was the reunion with his two youngest children who had made the journey with us.

London. England. My first daylight sight was of an enormous train station the colour of soot and huge trains of a not dissimilar state. Travelling at high speed we arrived in Birmingham at a station called Snow Hill. To my surprise the station looked the same as the one we had left behind. My uncle ushered us into a large, black car. I was reluctant to enter. This was a funeral car - a hearse no less. Why? I soon learnt that it was a hired car called a taxi. As we drove along, the majority of the buildings seemed to be identical and were full of soot. What a dirty, drab place this was and it wasn't even winter. We came to a long road on which all the buildings were of red bricks and joined to each other. They all sported chimneys. Now at least there was something I recognised. In St. Kitts my village had a communal oven, it was the only place I'd seen a chimney. This must be the street of all the

bakeries. Here must be the place where the bread for all of
England was baked. Delighting in the recognition I proudly
declared to my uncle, "What a lot of ovens they have in
England."

He laughed heartily and said, "No darling, these are what
we live in!"

Soon we were walking into one of these red-bricked oven
houses. Sure enough it was a house but not what I'd expected.
My uncle, his wife and their children - of which there were
four - were going to live in two rooms. This was not the England
I'd read about in history books. England was supposed to be
an affluent place. Why were they living like this?

Night-time descended much later than expected. By six in
St.Kitts, except for the moonlight nights, it would be dark
outside. This was indeed a strange place. An adult male cousin
- who had been in England some three years - arrived and we
were sent off with him along the road to another red brick
house for the night. To my surprise we were not only expected
to share the same room but also the same bed. When I was
younger I had slept with other children, but in recent years my
bed was my own and as far back as I can remember I had
always had my own bedroom. Life in England was proving to
be full of the unexpected. I wasn't unhappy. I was simply
surprised.

My mother and I continued to sleep with my cousin for
about a week whilst accommodation was sought for us. Mother
registered at the Labour Exchange and had been found a
factory job and was now well occupied during the day. Each
morning after breakfast I would make my way along the rows
of red-bricked houses to pass the day with my two cousins.

A week in an enclosed space is an oppressive environment
for children who are unaccustomed to spending their life cooped
up indoors. I was therefore delighted to learn that the following
week I would be taken to school.

As I walked the long drive to my new school I was indeed impressed. It was the biggest, newest and cleanest building I had seen since my arrival. It was set in pleasant grounds along a leafy road. This is more like it, I thought to myself. It was almost the end of summer term but nevertheless they accepted me and, to my surprise, without any examination to assess my abilities, they placed me in a class. Where I came from any child who had previous schooling was always tested. My capabilities were never assessed, either then or in September when the new year began.

There were just under 900 pupils in the school. I was overwhelmed by the sheer numbers and noise as we moved from room to room and the boisterousness of the children. I was the only black child, or 'coloured' as we were called then, in a class of 38. Previously in St.Kitts I went to a small fee-paying school where the teachers' attention was almost always available and we pupils respected our teachers. In this new setting, respect for teachers had not been inculcated. Thus whilst attempting to teach the class, their attention was regularly diverted by disinterested clusters of pupils who made no distinction between behaviour in the classroom and the playground. I was afraid of some of these children and they were all white! The white people I had previously had contact with prior to my arrival in England were generally financially well-off and with few exceptions presented themselves in a better light. I was shocked by this 'new breed'.

In the interim my home life in this new country was taking shape. Within ten days of arrival my mother and I had moved into our first room - 167 Alcester Road - our first home in England, our own address at last. It was a large, Victorian four-bedroomed house in a pleasant district. I was now adjusting fast and no longer imagined that I would have my own room, it was enough to share a room just like my mother. This house belonged to a Jamaican couple who, like the rest of us, lived in one room, with the household sharing one bathroom and kitchen. There were twelve occupants in the house, the two reception rooms were also being rented. We were a motley crew indeed: Jamaicans, Kitticians and Barbadians all under one roof. Then we still held very distinct identities based on the islands from which we had emigrated.

There were many positive factors attached to living in this house. The owners were childless and took great pleasure in indulging we children who lived there. It provided easy access to my school, the shops and two big parks. Our lives changed rapidly and, since leaving St. Kitts, I had not played with my precious doll Barbara who travelled with us in her own exclusive suitcase. I was fast adapting to the new mode and pace of life. My appetite for childish things had been rapidly assuaged by the many tasks needed to be done in order for my mother and I to function as a reasonable family.

Amongst these was the need to console my mother in her deep sadness and loss at having had to leave the other children behind. Most evenings she was in tears and I tried my best to comfort her. I did not miss my siblings, perhaps because back home, I had for a number of years acted in *loco parentis* and due to this, I may have felt relieved of those responsibilities. Also, for the first time in my life I had my mother's exclusive attention and this pleased me, though nothing I did to ease her pain of loss seemed to help.

Life in Britain was a challenge and my mother was now questioning the wisdom of our venture. It therefore seemed imperative that I did whatever was within my power to ensure that we made a success of the journey on which we'd embarked. This meant that overnight I was forced to grow up - a corollary of which was the great sense of importance I experienced as we joined forces against the odds.

So what did this entail for me? My mother and I would shop on Friday evenings for food and as the week elapsed I would supplement this, buying such items as bread, fresh fish and paraffin. It was my responsibility to clean our room and the communal area, upon which we agreed. I cooked all our evening meals except Sundays which was always special. Cooking was not always a straightforward matter as it meant sharing a four-ringed gas cooker with at least six other people. I soon experienced that as a child, the adults expected me to wait until they had finished. I was having none of that. I was acting on my mother's behalf. I too had inserted my penny in the gas meter and had the same rights to use the cooker. I soon won respect for my ability to stand up for myself and before long everyone was giving me tips on gravy preparation and the likes. However, the best times were when I would rush home from school and have the kitchen all to myself. I would prepare our meal then take it to our room to keep it warm on the paraffin heater until Mother arrived.

This first summer in England was a shock as it was unlike any other I had known. Back in the Caribbean I would spend some of my holidays helping in my grandmother's shop, dressing the window, sorting out boxes, being praised and pampered by the minute. Now I received weekly letters from her. We were both desperately missing each other and she was in the shop alone. Part of my summer would also have been spent on my uncle's farm with my siblings and cousins. I loved being on the farm. Us children would wander off to the beach, into the mango groves, or hang precariously from a bedroom window picking ripe plums when we were supposed to be having our afternoon siesta. Instead, here I was in Birmingham, spending hours alone or going to our adult Kittician friends and passing the day in their company indoors.

My mother insisted that I was not allowed to go to the park without an adult accompanying me as she feared for my life. This injunction was apparently due to an eleven-year-old Brownie who had disappeared (and was possibly murdered) on her way home from a pack meeting. Thus for the first couple of years, my mother viewed England as a dangerous place for children. I can clearly remember one evening returning about five minutes late from an errand only to see in the distance my mother, standing in front of the house crying as she feared that someone had taken me away.

Like many other Caribbeans we longed to see the ocean. It had been a daily feature of our life back home. Various inter-island organisations arranged a day trip to Western-super-mare. When we got there, what was pointed out to us as the ocean was unlike anything we had ever seen before. A grey, dirty mass of sand and sludge miles away and the English driver trying his best to explain the fluctuation of the tide in this part of the world. We were, of course, disappointed as we always associated the sea with a deep, blue colour. Nevertheless we huddled together reminiscing on 'back home' and 'these strange people and their cold country'. We feasted on our communal picnic and laid siege to the souvenir shops.

September 1960 saw the arrival of five other black children at school. With the exception of one child, who like me had not long arrived from the Caribbean, the others had spent most of their life in England.

It was about this time that I was first called 'wog' and told 'to go back home'. I always gave the impression that I had not heard but inwardly I was smarting with anger and pain. Racism was not yet a word I was familiar with. Playtime - or recess as we referred to it back home - was during my first year great moments of isolation. Boys and girls had separate playgrounds and girls quickly paired off with each other from the class or sought friends from their previous school. Apart from using the toilets and making necessary purchases for refreshments at the tuck shop we were all expected to spend what seemed like interminable amounts of time outside without our coats irrespective of the weather. The classrooms were locked. As winter descended this whole playtime routine seemed quite barbaric and I yearned for the relative comfort of my desk near the radiator.

I soon realised that I was not engaging in the general activities in the class. I was in essence bored and upset that I had been demoted. I soon realised that the English did not know how to write or speak their language properly.

Back home I was used to such poets as Browning, Walter de la Mare and of course Shakespeare. No foreign languages were spoken in my class whereas back home I was a reasonable student at French. I resented the fact that I had been placed in that school without even being assessed. Therefore I passed a lot of time physically in the classroom but mentally elsewhere.

I had always been a lover of nature. In the Caribbean we had always grown fruits and vegetables. Now from September onwards I was experiencing a vivid drama of nature each day. This was autumn. The magical changing of the leaves leading to the eventual nakedness of the trees and with it came frost. At the same time my mother and I were well equipped with winter blankets, flannelette sheets, coats and paraffin heater for our room. All of these things were entirely new to me and the latter pieces of equipment were to play a central role in my life, as each winter I became ill with what was commonly known as 'paraffin bronchitis'. There I would lay alone in a cold room in the empty, dark house waiting for my mother to return from work.

As winter dragged on, irrespective of how long we burned the paraffin heater, our room was always cold. Most evenings my mother and I would take it in turns to iron our clothing in order to warm our bodies or I would lay with my head under the blankets in order to generate extra warmth. One evening we explained this situation to a Caribbean visitor who looked about the room and explained that it was damp and therefore not a good long-term environment for us. His point was confirmed when the following summer we resurrected our lightweight clothing from the boxes under our bed only to find that they were damp with mildew. It was time to find a new room.

According to Caribbean adults finding work was not a problem, but finding a room was another thing. How right they were. As soon as I knew that we would need a home I began reading the noticeboards in Moseley Village where we lived. Many rooms were advertised and the occasional flat. However, almost all of them said, 'No blacks, No Irish, No dogs' and some went on to say 'No children'! I soon gave up my search for a home on the noticeboard in Moseley Village and realised that a room would be found through sharing our plight with other islanders.

Of all the trauma I suffered as a child in England, the need to find a comfortable room was always the most painful and disruptive. Between the ages of 11 and 19 our family moved seventeen times! It caused me many moments of acute embarrassment and fear, traces of which still remain with me today.

I simply dreaded Friday nights. That was the time when rent was paid and notices delivered. In the '60s many people were still coming to England and landlords felt a responsibility to their new arriving relatives and friends. Initially this was the main reason why we moved with such regularity. Also, sometimes the landlords themselves, having lived in one room, suddenly felt the need for a little more room for themselves in which they and their family could 'stretch out their legs.' In giving us notice, they were always very apologetic, but this did not ease the embarrassment of being forced to lead such an itinerant lifestyle.

I was already conspicuous in my class at school due to my skin colour and accent. My difference was further highlighted by my frequent change of addresses. I had to inform the teacher and of course the class register only had space for one change of address in any one year. I changed addresses several times and found it extremely embarrassing. Teachers became annoyed because the lack of space in the register required them to do extra work to sort out the formalities. I often mused on what the other children thought regarding me and my family moving so often. Did they think we had reneged on our rent? Did they think there was something dreadfully wrong with us? What did they think when I no longer walked home with them after school but went in the opposite direction? Apart from my concerns about what my English friends thought, I held a much deeper fear. What would happen if we had to leave an address and had nowhere to go? What would we do? I feared that we would end up sleeping on the streets or under a bridge. I wished we could find words to inform our relatives back home of what life was really like here, but what was the point? In those early days, we were totally unaware of the services offered by the local council. No one thought to fill us in with this information and so my mother and I simply knuckled down and made the most of the situation in which we had unknowingly placed ourselves.

No matter how little my mother earned, she always managed to save some of her earnings - even when it was £4.10 and our rent was 30 shillings she still saved. This meant that by the end of three years she could dry her tears and send for my brother and sister to join us.

The impending arrival of my siblings did not delight me. It had, at times, been very difficult to find a suitable room for two people; now we were knowingly putting more strain on ourselves by having two extra people in one room. I was now a teenager and wanted to have some privacy. How would four of us manage in one room? I kept these thoughts from my mother, for I knew that we would be one family again and it would ease my mother's aching heart.

A single fold-up bed was purchased for my brother. When not in use for sleeping purposes it was folded into a small table which served a variety of uses. My mother, my sister and I crammed into the double bed at nights in the small attic room in which we lived. Overnight my mother was a transformed woman - all her three jewels were once again together. She was a happy mother at last.

I was now fourteen but still felt no real affinity with any individual or groups of children at school except when on the sports field. I continued to loathe playtime and long lunch breaks for it was at such times that I felt most alone, most isolated. It was then that I felt my difference, not just amongst my white peers but also the few black girls with whom I'd become acquainted. With the exception of one black pupil they all seemed to behave in much the same way as their white peers. This pupil had, like myself, spent her early years in the Caribbean, but, unlike myself, she was prepared to meet fire with fire and our white counterparts were igniting the sparks as more and more black children were entering the school. This girl became my ally and would deal verbally and physically with trouble-makers in a way I could not. But the name-calling and bullying went on much the same without teachers ever addressing the problem. The maxim seem to be to ignore it and it will go away. They seemed not to realise that black children and black people had a right to be in England.

It was about this time that I took on a paper round at a local newsagent and was enjoying being outdoors in the early mornings. I later learned that a young man at school, one of the racists, had lost this position to me and he would travel some distance to harass me on my round. From the outset, I decided that I would not respond verbally but neither would I show any sign of fear, and I certainly had no intention of giving up my paper round. The war of attrition continued for several weeks until one day he no longer appeared. I could only assume he became exhausted and realised I was not going to concede. This 'little black bastard,' as he referred to me, 'who had stolen his bleeding job' was here to stay.

Weekends for a black child growing up in the sixties in a large city such as Birmingham was a time of excitement. There was always someone getting married, there was always a party to attend. Most Saturdays we would be surrounded by scores of Caribbean people, we would see and hear ourselves reflected back. All ages would gather under one roof, we would dance, tell stories, catch up on news from back home and other parts of the world where our people had settled. Those were some of the happiest times in my childhood.

By the time I was fifteen I was ready to leave school - legally I could. However, my mother's word was to be respected and I acted upon it; I therefore stayed on until I was almost seventeen, during which time I took commercial studies which included shorthand and typing. When I went out into the world to earn my living I was grateful for my mother's advice and firm insistence. Even though it was not my intention to pursue this as a means of earning a living, it was a good springboard which served me well.

My childhood in England was not what I had expected it to be. I felt that my family and I were at times creatively meeting the difficulties as best as we could. It was akin to being in the middle of a battle and responding as positively as possible under fire. Such experiences condition one and leave marks on the psyche.

As an adult I have consciously created a lifestyle which had its core time for introspection - specifically in the form of reflection and meditation. This has enabled me to assess what the gains and losses have been as a result of the major up-heaval and to some extent do some reparative work for the eleven year old girl who lost her childhood in that creative battle.

Muditasri

DECLAN JOSEPH

Declan Joseph came to England aged ten. He enjoys
writing and reading his poetry. He is an accomplished
musician who plays the guitar. He sometimes
accompanies his poetry with music.

The Unsung Journey

The unsung journey from the Caribbean was unpredict able. The ship's luxurious surroundings were something new to me, and so enjoyable that I couldn't help feeling that life in England would be promising. I was ten years old and the arrival of a young, West Indian boy into a new and well-developed country presented a challenge which I felt would surely pave the way to an adulthood of great wealth and higher intellect.

The 1960s in London, England proved to be a fairytale of wonder, but the packages that presented themselves were not always wrapped with a red ribbon.

The first generation that came was made up in the majority by poor people from the rural areas of the Caribbean - with a few professionals thrown in amongst them. They found work for example with the catering companies such as Lyons, Peak Frean or Hayward Military Pickle factory to name a few. They offered work to the most unskilled, men and women alike. There was no discrimination. There was no need to discriminate, for these thankless low paid jobs were only available to us because white people did not want these jobs and because of the labour shortage left after the war.

Let's look at the facts. The people who arrived here in those early days were mostly uneducated. They came to fill a gap. They mostly used the skills they had arrived with, carpenters for example, or worked as labourers. If they were fortunate enough to be exempt from the family responsibilities of bringing up children, they could improve their prospects by going to night school. In spite of these shortcomings, laziness in those days did not exist. Our parents went through a time of competitive zeal. They worked hard. They did not depend on the welfare state, to the extent that we do today. Every family was obsessed with working in order to purchase and secure a house, which was unbelievably cheap in those days. The home was for the family they intended to have or for those they already had and was saving to bring over from the Caribbean. They wanted to give us the opportunities that they never had. We were their offspring. We came over to join them and it wasn't easy, but they knew that an even better future awaited us, who came after them, because they knew that everything was better here, especially the schooling.

This was of course one of the things that made us feel a sense of belonging and a liking for this country - the superior education system. They made it known to us children that this was the best reason for leaving their homeland. They promoted the British education to us. If that did not suffice, then nothing would because as they discovered, the streets were certainly not paved with gold.

The chance to mix with the English proved to be very attractive. We did not co-habit much in those days, but there was definitely a sense of neighbourliness and respect, the likes of which I had not experienced before and would not experience again.

We found the English way of life satisfying and participated fully. Above all we revelled in the new inventions, mechanical and electrical that England had to offer. The generation of the sixties was on a special kind of high, having come from a life of poverty and undeveloped countries - we were swept away by what to us was a high-tech society.

We had a black and white television which offered up a gem of programmes. I liked them all, especially the Westerns which kept my interest. We couldn't believe we were living on the same streets, or next door to white people, which proved to be a welcomed, entertaining and readily acceptable experience. Back home the whites were in the ruling minority. They kept themselves locked away in their ivory towers. We longed to be like them. To have what they had.

The only way we differed from them now was in the music. We had the 'Blue Spot' stereo units, and other styles of music system which made our way of life in the seventies a thing to be jealous of. Boy did the seventies prove to be a musical era of change and enjoyment.

> Joy to the world, all the boys and girls.
> Joy to the fishes in the deep blue sea
> Joy to you and me...

The promotion of Reggae at the time was welcomed and enjoyed by whites and black. It dampened down some of the prejudices and brought people together. It was in the music that we saw the acceptance of some of our people, and some managed to rise to the top in this industry. However the music also brought out differing attitudes in the English. If they liked your music you were alright, but if they did not like it, then you would feel the sting of not being fully appreciated and this took the form of racial abuse and even violence by whites on blacks.

Our music gave a lot to the British way of life. As a result we found ourselves getting into the society through the back door. Music created an incentive for afro integration. Of all the minorities here, our people and culture were the favourite amongst the English and very soon with all this integrating we saw the coming of mixed race babies.

By the '80s the English way of life had been so widely adopted by us, that all sense of values that we came with and should have retained have now been - if not lost, virtually owned by others. Youth culture as we know it today is recognisably black, but not necessarily owned, controlled or profited by us.

A lot of us who came here have gained economic and material privileges. Some of us have made it, but on the other hand many of us experience untold stress, mental illness, degradation, police brutality, deaths in custody, deaths on the street. The majority of our elders, if they were smart, would have returned home by now - but some remained locked in old people's homes - removed from their culture with nothing to look forward to here.

Those of us who came here as children are the older generation now. We try to hang on to what little we can remember of home so we can pass it on to our children. We ask ourselves can we go back, can we ever go back or do we like it here so much? This is the challenge that faces us. Things are no longer cheap, the whites have a monopoly on everything and the order of the day is to work hard so you can command the income that will afford you all the comforts of the material world. We also have the offsprings to think about. We have a duty to them, we have a role in shaping their future.

So we take stock of everything that has gone before and what will be, in the future and we are forced to realise that no matter where we are, in our lives or geographically, we are very much involved in the shaping of the modern world. We must remember that things change; people change; the world change, but we cannot control it. We can never control it.

Declan Joseph

ZINDIKA KAMAUESI

I grew up in Jamaica and Britain. I was brought up by a number of relatives and the community. Early movement in my childhood I feel has given me the independent, travelling and restless soul that I have.

I enjoy the writings of James Baldwin for his power and passion and Toni Morrison for her beauty and craft - a perfect combination to which I aspire
in my own writing.

Relative Strangers

*"The most valuable lesson I learned is when you address
a people by their right name, that name must relate to land,
history and culture. All people go back to a geography of
their original origin and identity no matter where they live
on the face of the earth. We have over-used the word black.
Black tells you what you look like - but it don't tell you
who you are. We are the only people who seems to have
lost that all essential trait of geographical and historical
reference."*

John Henrik Clarke - *A Great and Mighty Walk*

T he Caribbean family of which I am a product has al
ways intrigued me and in my childhood I observed the
relationship between men and women with curiosity.
The women were hard-working. They had children, reared
them, washed, cooked and cleaned and often worked outside
of the home; whereas the men were free to roam and roam
they did. I remember spending time in the house of a family
with eleven children, mainly girls. Their father had migrated to
England many years earlier and never returned or sent for
them as he had promised. A photo of the man, surrounded by
his children and wife, took pride of place in the house. The
mother of the family was a matriarch in the strongest sense,
and her older daughters were mini-matriarchs. Their house
stood on a hill, overlooking a valley spreading out into a green
wilderness and then up to meet the azure skyline. In the yard

were orange trees, mango trees and lime trees all laden with fruits. The house was always full of children because the older girls had grown up and were having children of their own. My favourite was Heather, who was like a mother to me. She combed my hair, plaited it and oiled my skin and she told me duppy stories.

Although coming from a respectable family, Heather was renowned for having one, then two, then three children with not a father in sight. She told me that a stork had come in the middle of the night and dropped the babies on top of the house. I was none the wiser until I grew older and realised that the stork were the men who called on her for the pleasures of night and were away before dawn. One day, whilst walking to the market town with Heather and her children, she waved to a man across the street. He waved back. 'That's my baby father,' she told me. Which baby I did not know. I just knew that this man was like a complete stranger to her and her children. From my childhood viewpoint, I observed Heather with admiration and pity. It seemed as if her relationships with men were something conducted only in the seclusion of darkness; that she often colluded in her own mistreatment and why were her 'babyfathers' complete strangers to their children, I wondered. Heather was a dutiful woman who carried out her work diligently in the community as a daughter, mother and surrogate mother who looked after other people's children like myself, but I don't ever recall seeing her smile.

Having strangers as family is not unusual in the Caribbean. It was not unusual for a man to have several families living in close proximity to each other in the same district. Migration was sometimes a precursor to this arrangement. Margaret Prescod addressed the issue in her book *Bringing It All Back Home*:

"Quite often the men would come over and maybe leave

*a family in Barbados, but pick up with another woman in
London, New York, to reproduce them and start another
family. So when the men went by themselves, you were
taking a chance. Your best bet was to get a woman to go
because you knew that a woman was tied to her housework
- the housework of reproducing her kids back home. The
man was a different story. Sometimes in the village there
would be occasions when Mr so and so would come back
from England and he would bring his new wife and child.
But meanwhile, Mr so and so had a woman and two
children up the road. That was quite common."*

This issue of fragmentary family pattern and separation is
one that concerns me and so when I began my research on
the topic I immediately went in search of a book I came across
in 1985 called *'My Mother Who Fathered Me'* which left a
lasting impression on me. The book was published in 1954 and
in it the author, Edith Clarke, studied family life in three
Jamaican districts. I was attracted to the book because of the
title, which I found fascinating and profound. In its simplicity;
it seemed to sum up black Caribbean family life as one that
was largely matriarchal with an absent or weak father role.

Clarke identified three family types, which remain pertinent
today:
1. Christian Marriage - based on conjugal and domestic union
formally entered into in the manner prescribed by the law.
(This practice is adhered to by the white upper class and
adopted by the brown middle class).
2. Common Law Marriage or Concubinage - the union of man
and woman which lasts indefinitely without the full sanction of
the law.
3. Woman-centred households which may consist of a single
mother or the extended female family members. (Households
2 and 3 usually consist of the half siblings from previous unions

and are found mainly amongst the black, poorer class, who are in the majority).

Clarke uses the term 'concubinage' to refer to the practice of a cohabiting man and woman, usually resulting in the getting of children, but is not recognized in the legal sense and so there is no safeguard for the woman or her children when the union ends. If and when she enters into another conjugal union, she may find she is unable to have all her children with her. Thus siblings and half siblings were separated and often distributed among a number of widely scattered households. With such variations in family life, children were often subjected to disruption at any moment from their closest kin. Clarke points out that this was a general rather than a unique or individual experience, however, the effects of instability in the relationship between parents did have a profound effect on the development of parent-child roles and particularly between father and child.

As we can see, from Clarke's study, movement is not an unusual part of a Caribbean childhood. Often, children are sent from country to town or town to country to live with relatives and friends. Haphazard family life and a state of fatherlessness, has undoubtedly left many black children with a deep sense of loss, which is rarely acknowledged. But the bewilderment of being sent on a plane or a boat, as a MTA (Minor Travelling Alone) to the other side of the world, only to be met by relative strangers is something we care not to dwell on.

Many of us who came to England as children experienced loss which we were never able to verbalise and many parents discounted the fact that their children could have any such feelings, thereby taking away the opportunity to heal. When I talk with people who have had this experience, we inevitably focus on the gap between leaving and arrival, the casting off, of one life to start another. We talk about the rejection we faced from the wider society and our response to this was to reject the society and our parents who seemed to accept it so readily. Our parents were of a different mindset. They had left worse behind. We grew up here and felt entitled, but never got. With hindsight, many of us hit out at the system in ways that were self-destructive. All this flew in the face of parents who were hard-working, religious and wanted the best for their children. We talk about our alienation and the extent of our trauma has never being fully recognised. We talk about the pain of forgetting and only daring to remember twenty or thirty years later when we return back home for the first time.

Our separation was not only from kith and kin, but also from a land and a climate. Most of us who came here were rural people confined to an urban landscape. In Britain, we have become fearful of the countryside. Yet, we have always been rural people. We hunted, fished, planted, raised cattle in Africa and made our houses from what the land gave us. We worked the fields and cut sugarcane, enslaved in the West. We were given a plot of land on emancipation, which we continued to farm and pass down the generations to this day. We went from the sunshine to fog and snow. How has environmental displacement affected our mind, body and spirit? Do we die younger? Do we suffer from depression, mental illness and cold related illnesses more? Who knows? Does anyone care? I know my skin is pale from the lack of sunshine and vitamin D and in the winter I am as gloomy as the tree outside my window that has lost all its leaves. In winter a bird sometimes perches on the naked branch and I am reconnected with nature. Perhaps, when I travel to the Lake District and English seaside towns, what I am really searching for are the sights and sounds of my childhood.

Of course, migration is a necessary evil, which we all crave in a romantic sort of way. We like to spread our wings and explore, but inevitably, it means separation in a manifold sense. When we left Grandmother behind, we were bereft of a whole generation, their wisdom and their knowledge. Auntie going to

Canada, and Uncle to America further fractured the extended family. Even if we ended up in the same country, we might be at different ends and not aware of each other.

The older generation who came here are now retiring back home which means that yet another generation of youngsters will grow up without the wisdom and cultural connection which grandparents brings. The importance of the oral tradition will be lost if it is not passed on from grandparents to grandchildren. Grandparents are an important link to our past, yet many of us, do not know them or only see them when we return home to bury them. When you migrate it is even more important that rituals are kept, but the very act of migrating forces you to take on a bit of other people's culture and in the process, you lose a bit of yourself. How much you lose or give away, depends on your tenacity to uphold, embrace and cherish the fact that you are different, and your history is elsewhere, your lineage is elsewhere, your race is elsewhere; everything that is you, reflects you and represents you is elsewhere.

Heather was my surrogate mother, yet if I saw her today in the street I would not recognise her or her me. Yet, I was close to her, but we lost touch. Heather lost her father to migration and her children were separated from their fathers and so the culture of disconnection and procreation without responsibility goes on. A legacy of distrust, disloyalty and disunity divide us, and black men continue to desert their women and children in droves.

Today I see young boys on the street - they are desperate for fathers or something. They are lost for role models, lost for that true sense of a caring masculinity rather than a ruthless one. There is disrespect in their posture, they have a don't care attitude, but if you look beyond that, you will see that they are mere children uncertain of how to be. Sometimes that deficiency in their parenting is made up by outside forces. Children, they say, will follow in their fathers' footsteps. If there are no fathers they will follow in the footsteps of others, the gansta rapper, the drug dealer or the gunman. Plenty of girls I notice are pregnant at the same young age their mothers were and they will be the single mothers of tomorrow. Forty-one percent of single mothers struggle on in adversity, being both mother and father to their children. This is further complicated today not only by the fathers being absent from the home, but also the mothers having to work long unsociable hours and going further and further afield to find work in order to fill the gap left by men.

But, we were not always like this. Among this erosion, there was a brief hiatus, which may have gone unnoticed.

Let me take you back to the classroom of the seventies. Nearly everyone I knew at school had a mum and a dad. We mostly came from two parent families. Some of these fathers were strict, Victorian-like in stature, partial to beating and over zealous about religion and their approach to education. The Windrush generation as they are called did create a sense of family based on marriage. Some of these marriages may have been forced by the exigency of migration - but they were a family nonetheless. Ironically, migration did split the family - but it also ended up creating a sense of partnership between women and men. The men for a change, found a purpose, they were working hard and saving to send for their wife, children, to buy a house - migration forced responsibility on them never before seen. Not all were able to live up to this responsibility and forgot about back home - but those who took on the challenge saw that all things were possible in England that were not possible in the Caribbean. They were no longer peasants and colonial subjects despite racism they were truly free men - England would allow them to pursue their dreams.

How could we have known that sadly, this dream would be lost on ensuing generations? We have become a community plagued by many social problems. We have lost the cohesiveness we once had as a people and we have become individualistic, blase and distant. I can't help thinking is this because we are trapped in the wrong hemisphere and living a life out of sync? Many of us are blinkered or even blind to the fact that migration has impacted hard on our psyche and spirit. We think only of the economic wealth and material benefits. Much like a mother who buys her child the latest name brand and gadget but fails to show it affection and attention. So too, migration with all its trappings, fools us into thinking we are better off, when in fact, we are not. Migration eats away at our soul and our self-respect. It takes away our identity and our dreams crumble. It leaves us in a state of bereavement - a ghost of our former self.

It has been many years since I left Jamaica and I now return for holidays. I am reunited with the land of my birth and I am suddenly aware of its abundant beauty. I realise that here, even the poorest can own a piece of real estate, which we could never have in England.

Picture an idyllic beach scene in Jamaica. The sand is white and soft; the palm trees are swaying in the light breeze. I am standing on the beach paddling and the turquoise sea is rushing in to nuzzle my bare feet. I am at peace. I am rested. I am relaxed. I relish the reconnection; the wellness I feel.

My mood and my memories from the ancestors tell me that we were not always like this - people with problems. That we did have values, rituals, customs, and a system, which we need to reclaim in order to bolster ourselves. My mood and my memories tell me that, only when we find our true nature, can we redeem ourselves and rid ourselves of the violence and self-hatred that negate and eat away at our spirit, our humanity and our communities. Only through reconnection and responsibility can we bring about our redemption.

Zindika Kamauesi

Quotes taken from:
1. Margaret Prescod, *Black Women: Bringing it all back home* (Falling Wall Press)
2. Edith Clarke, *My Mother Who Fathered Me - A study of family life in three selected Jamaican communities.* (Allen & Unwin, 1954)

The Meaning of the Journey
(Interviews)

The early passport pictures have now faded. The
children are now the parents. They are the adults of
today. We are looking back in order to look forward.
Where are we now? What does the future hold?

As this book draws to a close, it is time to reflect.
With reflection comes questions. Was the journey
worthwhile? What did we gain? What did we lose? The
biggest question is one of identity and belonging. Who
are we? Where do we belong? Will we ever go back or
is Britain truly home?

Our parents extolled the virtues of a good education
and some of us succeeded. Despite the odds, many have
made good careers and have privileged lifestyles. Our
aspirations were not just individualistic. Unlike our
parents we didn't want to just survive - we wanted to
make a change, one that would bring fruition for the next
generation and the next. We have a lot to celebrate, but
what about the losses.

We were the first significant number of black children
to be educated in Britain and as such we were the guinea
pigs. For some, a good education still eludes. In *'Roots
to Success'*, Lloyd Marshall talks about the particular
challenge that we still face in educating the black child
in Britain. "The first generation were in awe of the
British Education system - but now we have a situation
whereby, the second generation (parents of the boys who
are currently coming to school) did not have a positive
experience of school in England and they relay their
unhappiness to their children. Parents have to be in there
supporting and cajoling their children and unfortunately
there are many black parents who are unable to do that."

The education of black boys looks very bleak. There

is a sense of deja-vu. There is a feeling that we might have been running on the spot. There is also a feeling that we might not fit in anywhere else because we have lived here for too long. Some feel they have invested too much in British society to leave. We have come too far to go back now and the younger generation know no other home.

For many of us though, the journey back home is the solution. There we are in the majority and we are surrounded by people who look like us. The pace of life is slower and we live in harmony with the environment which is attractive. Angela Gay made the big step. For her England was not a bed of roses, never was and never would be. In 1985 she went home to Barbados. "I hated the way of life in England. I hated the racism. I hated not feeling like I belonged."

Lloyd Marshall also talks about wanting to give something back to the country he came from as a reason he might eventually return. Annette Sylvester, *'The Meaning of the Journey'* feels that too much has been lost to Britain and we need to look elsewhere for our future. We should be contributing to the prosperity of our own countries. She is still searching for a home other than Britain.

Undoubtedly we have changed British society a whole lot - but it has also changed us. We were the wide-eyed children who made the first journey, but now we are adults with a foot in both camps. We are the crossover generation.

The pieces herein offer many conclusions to the journey and its meaning. For many the pursuit of education and a strong identity is tantamount to living in England. Others find strength in travel, creativity and the fact that we were not born in this land, means there is somewhere else we call home.

LLOYD VAN MARSHALL

Lloyd Van Marshall was born in Jamaica. He came to
England to join his parents when he was nine years old.
Lloyd is the Headmaster of Dulwich High School for Boys,
a comprehensive school situated in the wealthy middle-class
area of Dulwich Village. Lloyd is married with three
children. He lives in London.

From Roots to Success

I was born in St.Thomas, a Parish on the Eastern seaboard of Jamaica. My father left for England in the early fifties when I was about two years old. My, mother left in 1957 to join him. I then stayed with my grandmother until 1960 when I came to England.

Spare the Rod and Spoil the child

My grandmother was from the old school - spare the rod and you spoil the child - and there was no room for manoeuvre. So by the time I arrived in England to join my parents that principle of being disciplined was stamped on my backside, and the same expectations were there from my parents. My parents, like many first generations, were in awe of the British education system. Schooling in England was free and great things were expected of me. I don't think they appreciated the trauma that I had to go through, to cope with all that was being thrown at me from fellow students as well as the teachers. I had gone to an elementary school in St. Andrews, a school with a mixture of young people, representing the ethnicity of the Island, 'out of many one people'. There were many different youngsters there: Chinese, Syrian, Indian; in fact we were living next door to a German family and their children were at the same school. So in terms of the elementary schooling back home - colour prejudice wasn't really on the agenda.

In England, for the first time, I was made to feel that I was different. I became conscious of colour. Going home and sharing my experiences with my father and mother, they made

it clear to me that I was not going to school to like anyone or to
be liked by anyone; but to get an education. When you pass
your exams no one can take away your achievements. That
was the message. It was a hard message but I had to learn it.

As a child I found myself in a very loose and liberal schooling
system. Youngsters swore at and hit the teachers. I'd never
experienced anything like that in my schooling in Jamaica. I
soon realised that the lessons taught were well below my ability.
I had been far in advance in my schooling in Jamaica and I
thought I was now doing baby work.

I have always had a desire to achieve academically from
an early age, and the discipline of life in Jamaica had set me in
good stead for that. Despite my difficult primary and secondary
experience, it was my driving ambition to go to University and
be successful in my chosen career. One of the things that
helped to confirm that in my mind happened in the mid-sixties
when a young man came from Jamaica and lived in our house.
He was in his twenties and came to study law. He was black
and he was going to be a barrister!

**For the first time I thought here was somebody who I
could really look up to. He was my mentor.**

I thought, if he can do it, so can I. He was of tremendous
support. He was able to help with my school work and what I
admired in him most was the fact that he was a black man.

His mother had died when he was young and my mother
died when I was twelve. I thought , if he managed to overcome that bereavement, so could I. It was a tremendous boost,
having him there.

In my latter years at school I thought about what I wanted
to do. I thought about medicine, law and education. In the end
education won.

Route to Success

I started off by going to Teachers' College in the Midlands. When I came back to London, I worked for a year, whilst deciding where to teach. I worked in a shoe shop on the Kings Road. This was very exciting at the time, seeing all the hip people in the seventies. They wanted me to stay on and train as a manager but I thought it would be a waste of three years studying. I went back to the ILEA for another grant to do another degree. They said to me "We have already spent X amount of money on you - we feel you should go out and teach. I'm sure there must be a school in London that needs your services" - to which I replied: "Find me one."

The weeks went by and eventually I got a letter from ILEA informing me that I should report to Henry Thornton School in Clapham. I saw the head teacher who said that he was looking for a maths teacher, but my degree was in economics. He said that with an economics background, I should be able to teach maths. I started off at Henry Thornton teaching mathematics, commerce and economics.

I climbed the promotion ladder rapidly.

I was made the head of year after about four years. This was a school with a large number of black and ethnic minority students and as the only black teacher in the school it was patently obvious that I was required to bring about some discipline.

When a vacancy came up in the pastoral side, the head invited me to apply for this vacancy. I said I didn't want to go down that route - I wanted to become the head of the economics department, but he insisted that he wanted me to take over the head of year group. So the last five years at Henry Thornton I was head of year. I then saw a post for Deputy Headship at my old school - Ernest Bevin - which had amalgamated with a local grammar school which I applied for and was successful.

*I was making excellent progress at Henry Thornton -
but I thought I would throw my hat in the ring and was
pleasantly surprised when I got the post.*

Shortly after my appointment the head pointed out that I
had not been selected because I was black, or because I was
an old boy at the school, but because I was a damn good
teacher. I worked at Ernest Bevin for ten years. I was appointed
to second deputy, then first Deputy Head.

My coming to Dulwich High School as Head was one of
these off-the-cuff applications again. During the four years
leading up to my appointment here I had been applying for
headships and lecturing posts in the United States and Caribbean. My father had retired back to Jamaica in 1983 and I felt
I needed to get closer to him. So I had sent off a number of
applications and had been short-listed for a few posts.

The most prestigious was with the United Nations Interna-
tional School in New York. I interviewed for the Principal and
was in the final three, but that wasn't to be. I hung on at Ernest
Bevin and the headship for the then William Penn School came
up. I started here as Head in Sept 1992 - realising that it was
going to be an enormous challenge. That is basically how I've
looked at these last five years - it's a challenge. When my
friends ask me how I'm enjoying being the head of Dulwich
High School, I tell them that I don't use the term enjoyment
about my work. It is a challenge trying to turn around something that was raw and rough. I make no apologies for saying
this, but when I first came here - William Penn was a social
club. I told the staff that I would need their help to turn it into
a school; and that is basically what I have been trying to do.
But it is very hard, because we have here at this school some
extremely challenging young people.

*Eighty-four per cent of the children here are from ethnic
backgrounds and a high percentage from single parent
homes.*

The school is in Dulwich but most of the children come from outside of the area; Brixton, Peckham, New Cross and further afield. We don't get any boys from the Village that come here. Many parents who send their children here do so because the school happens to be in a prestigious area. They don't want their children to go to the local school in their area. They hope that by sending them into Dulwich, they will stand a better chance.

However, the context in which we are working is not easy, although we have made significant progress. Those who knew the school before I came here will see that there have been some significant changes in the school - but we still have a long way to go. We are under special measures from the government and their hit squads who have been here for the last two years. We are struggling to recruit, although this year the figures have improved but we are still threatened with closure. We have also had some extremely negative reporting in the local press. It has been five years of constant battle to improve the image of the school. That was one of the reasons for the relaunch and to change the name. I've always wanted to change the name. At my first meeting with the governors, back in October, I told them if I had my way I would change the name, and give everyone a new emphasis, and a new start.

Do you think the children who came from the Caribbean had a better education than those born in Britain?

The vast majority of children who had previous schooling in the Caribbean are far in advance of British-born black children, despite the fact that there are social/economic problems and poverty in the Caribbean which often prevent children from going to school. If I go to the Caribbean and pick an average school student there, his or her knowledge will be far in advance of the students here. The reason for that is because the schooling in the Caribbean extracts a great deal more from the children. Discipline is the key and what we lack in many of our schools, but obviously discipline has to start at home. There is a close relationship between home and school in the Caribbean. If you blinked at school, your family knew that you blinked. Many black parents here send their children to school and leave it up to the school to manage that child. That may work in the Caribbean - but not in Britain. I say to those parents, if you leave it up to the school alone - your child will fail. We, as black parents, cannot allow the school to progress our children. We must be prepared to involve ourselves in that educational process.

The first generation were in awe of the British education system - but we now have a situation whereby the second generation (parents of the boys who are currently coming to the school) did not have a positive experience of school in England and they relay this unhappiness to their children.

Parents have to be in there supporting, cajoling their children and unfortunately there are many black parents who are unable to do that.

I must admit that I don't get enough parents coming into the school - but I say to them that there is always an open invitation to visit the school at any time. In fact I wrote to the parents asking them to come in and help support the children in reading and writing because we have an enormous problem with literacy in this school - a large percentage of the boys are below their chronological reading age. Some parents have taken it up.

What would be interesting would be to study those black children who have achieved well and to find out about their upbringing. What we hear often is that the vast majority of black boys are leaving school unable to do simple sums, unable to write a letter applying for a job, and their grammar is useless. I would like to find out about black boys who are successful -

why? Black girls generally do better than black boys - why? If it is a particular issue to do with boys education, then we have to look at strategies for raising boys' achievements.

As a result of underachievement some parents are deciding to send their children back home to be educated. What do you think of such ideas?

It's understandable although regrettable, because often they are sending the children to a place which is home for the parents - but not the children and they are sending them to whom? Friends, relatives, elderly grandparents. I understand they feel the British education system has failed them - but I believe that is not the answer...

. . . Perhaps they believe that the environment in the Caribbean will be more conducive to learning and to the development of a more positive black identity?

Yes. That is a big factor. The growing up that I did in England was with the background of knowing that I was a minority in a foreign country where the pigment of my skin was a problem to the host community. Having to deal with that and, at the same time, pursue my studies, was pretty heavy. Taking the pressure of racism is not easy and going to school in the Caribbean, one is free of that pressure. My parents told me categorically when I came here I had to make myself twice as good as my white friends. Even then you may find you still don't get the job, because of the colour of your skin.

I'll never forget that lesson, and it was such an enormous burden having to carry it around, but it spurred me on to improve my qualifications and I managed to get two first degrees and a masters degree - and that was only so I could keep ahead of the field. But to expect that of everyone is not on.

How do you see the future of education in Britain?

What I think we need is a government that is truly committed
to raising standards by properly resourcing the schools, not
just with books and computer equipment, but with enough human
resources so that relationships with young people can be built
within a safe and caring environment. They have to spend
money to make sure that the environment in which adults and
young people are working is pleasant. Many of our schools
are not pleasant places to be.

*The first task I have as Headmaster is to socialise these
boys. They have to be disciplined, because without discipline there is no order, and without order they cannot learn.
Secondly my staff and I have to teach them to read; thirdly
we have to give them access to the national curriculum;
and fourthly, and miraculously, they are expected to get
five GCSEs at grade C and above - absolutely ridiculous.*

All schools should have help in establishing order and to
create an environment in which teaching and learning can take
place before we can look at the impact in the classroom. I
believe the answer lies in the formative years of our children,
all children. We have to look at what I refer to as the domestic
curriculum in their formative years, 0-5. I believe in most black
families it is poor, it is unchallenging; so many of those children
are entering the education system at a disadvantage. We need
government help with proper well-funded nursery resources
so that all children have a chance. I think that would go along
way to improving the appalling literacy problem.

Any government who is serious about raising standards
must look to these things and be prepared to redirect resources,
because the future of the country depends on the expectation
of these young people going through schools. If we are going
to have a sector of the society who think they haven't got
equal access to things out there, they are going to rebel, so the

social cost to society is going to be high.

*When one focuses on the issue of the underachieve-
ment of black pupils particularly boys, we must ask - what
are we storing up for ourselves?*

If these young black men are leaving school and they are
unemployable, spending days wandering the streets and getting
into trouble... what are we storing up? When they explode
what will happen - another series of riots? That's what the
government should be mindful of. So I think rhetoric has to be
matched with resources if we are to see the quality and high
standards that they are talking about.

How do you see your own future?

My mother and father always drummed it into me that education
was the greatest gift that a family can bestow on their children.
Because once you have it, no one can take it away. This post
at Dulwich High School has overwhelmed me in trying to see
if I can create something permanent here, something that will
last, something that no one can take away. If we are able to
achieve that - fantastic. If we are not able to improve the
school sufficiently, then they will close it down.

As for myself, I have always felt that teaching was
something I could do anywhere as long as I can speak the
language. One day I might like to return to the Caribbean - but
I would definitely like to make a contribution to a developing
world economy, in the Caribbean or elsewhere. It is still my
intention to do so.

* *Unfortunately, Lloyd lost the battle to save Dulwich High
School for Boys. Since this interview the school has been closed
down.*

DENNIS MORRIS

Dennis Morris was born in Jamaica and brought
up in Hackney, London. He came to England
with his mother when he was five years old.
He is married with two children.

At the time of this interview, Dennis had a new exhibition
called 'Growing Up Black' at the Thom Blau Gallery in
Tower Bridge, London. The exhibition featured a
collection of unseen photographs that Dennis took in the
'70s. The pictures captured the diversity and experiences
of black life at the time: home life, blues dance,
church, sound systems, politics and reggae.
I went to see the exhibition and interviewed him
about his work.

Growing Up Black

Could you tell me why you wanted to do this exhibition at this time?

Because we have reached a time when there is a generation who need to see where they came from. They need to see how far we have come and how far we have to go. The generation now have it pretty easy. Many of them know about Stephen Lawrence, but before that, there were many Stephen Lawrences. They have a lot of freedom because of what we have gone through. The new immigrants also need to know what went on before they came. They only have the freedom and the rights they have, because of what we went through. There were times as a youth when I couldn't walk in the West End without being picked up by the police. The youths and the recent immigrants take all this for granted. They just need to be reminded or told about the good times and the bad - so I think the time is right for this exhibition.

The exhibition took a year to prepare. I have pictures taken over a period of 10 -15 years, so there was a lot to choose from. My favourite one is of the choir boys in church. Also, the one of the black guy and the white guy holding up a banner saying free all political prisoners, it seems as if they are talking, but the black guy is giving the white guy a really hard time. I like the one of Steel Pulse, the reggae band. It features two of the band members dressed in Ku Klux Klan gear, surrounded by the other members of the band. It is meant to depict the evil within our midst, but a lot of people don't like that picture. It is very controversial because of the image. There are a lot of subtleties in the pictures; that is why the exhibition is called

'Growing Up Black' because every picture has a story to tell.

So could you tell me a little of your story. How did a boy who was born in Jamaica, growing up in Hackney become a photographer?

As a kid in the early seventies, growing up black in England was a strange experience. At school we were always placed at the back of the class with no real attention paid to us or to our abilities. You had to struggle on your own to be heard or to achieve. Racism was everywhere, couched in cynical taunts: 'Wogs the matter, Dennis? Browned off? Nigger mind'. If you were to retaliate, however, you were invariably punished.

St. Marks Church, Dalston was my saviour in more ways than one. I was a member of the church choir, started by Reverend Donald Pateman who was the vicar. It was an unusual church at the time because the vicar was white, but the choirboys and the congregation were all black. The patron of the church was Donald Patterson - a famous inventor of photographic equipment. He ran a photo club for the choirboys and, through him, I discovered the magic of photography. The photo of the choirboys in church, I took that one when I was twelve years old.

Did you always want to be a photographer?

Yes, ever since I discovered photography at the age of nine. I also learned to develop and print. Mr Patterson saw my potential and took me under his wings and guided me. He was my mentor.

Do you think it is important to have mentors?

It was an important part of my growing up and achieving my

goals, especially for black youngsters at that time in the seventies. We were part of a first generation, getting ready to take our place in society, even if society was not ready for us. For many of us then, our talents remained largely ignored. As I reached school leaving age, my career officer asked me what I planned to make of my life. When I replied, 'to become a photographer' he told me that I was being silly - 'there is no such thing as a black photographer.' Sad that so many of us were given blinkered advice.

Every child needs a mentor. Someone they can trust, to nurture their potential. It could be their parents or someone outside of the family. Many black children don't have mentors in their family - so they have to look outside of the family for a role model.

Tell me a little about your route to success as a photographer?

My career wasn't planned. I discovered something I liked and I knew it was for me so I pursued it relentlessly, even though I was getting a lot of stick from my friends. I was obsessed with photography, when others of my peers were more interested in football, chasing girls, blues dances, nicking and fighting and generally getting themselves into trouble.

Every person finds their vocation in life sooner or later. Luckily I found mine sooner, at the age of nine. I read all the books, the magazines and got out there and took pictures. It was a natural part of my life. Nothing could distract me from it. Even my parents didn't know what to make of it, and even if they had said anything against it, it would not have stopped me.

Photography is my joy and passion. I have smashed cameras because I haven't captured what I saw through the lens. Anyone can take a picture, but to take a good picture, you need a third eye. I don't tell people what they should get from my pictures. I just know that when people see my pictures it evokes emotions in them.

There aren't many black photographers around, so do you see yourself as some kind of pioneer or even as you say, a mentor or role model for those starting out?

Yes, I am a pioneer, but at the same time I am not. There have always been black photographers around. I wasn't the first. There was a black photographer called Van der Zee in the 1900s. He documented the life of people in Harlem. There was also another supremely successful black photographer called Gordon Parks. He was the first black photographer to work for Time Life magazine, which was a very prestigious magazine. He went on to direct Shaft and Superfly. He is part of that whole black dynasty in America, alongside people like Bill Crosby and Quincy Jones.

I would like to think I'm a role model, although you wouldn't know I was a black photographer. I have worked with the Sex Pistols. The pictures I did of them are iconic. Through them I documented a whole generation. When people meet me they are baffled that a white band would have a black photographer. But, I am an artist first and I do the work I do because I am an artist. The fact that I am black is just a bonus.

My Sex Pistol pictures and Bob Marley pictures are the main work that people know me through. They say they are such great pictures. But they are surprised that I am black; they are saying they don't think a black person can take such great pictures. Even though Bob Marley was black they still think his photographer can't be black, and it is not just white people who think that, your own black people contradict you too. But, as I said, I am an artist. My tool is the camera, rather than the paintbrush or the chisel.

Did you receive any formal training?

I did go to college. I don't know what they made of me.

Why do you say that?

I mean, going to college took me back to square one. They were doing things that I'd already done at the age of nine. I knew the answer to a lot of things and I kept putting my hand up. They didn't like the fact that I knew so much. I left - or maybe they kind of threw me out. I didn't miss it. So you could say I was more or less self-taught, with the guidance of Mr. Patterson.

Tell me a little about some of your greatest achievements so far.

Well, I suppose I would have to put my Bob Marley and Sex Pistol pictures at the top. Also, photography has broadened my horizons and because of it, I have travelled far and wide. People see me as a successful photographer, but what is success? I would be more successful if I hadn't diverted from music to social documentary. I would have made more money in music. But I stuck to social documentary because that was what I set out to do from the start - social reportage was my style, and it was only through meeting Bob Marley that drew me into the music industry. Meeting Bob, combined my love of music and photography.

How did you meet Bob Marley?

I heard that he was playing at a place called the Speak-easy Club, so I bunked off school - and just waited for them to come along for a sound check. Eventually they turned up. Bob,

Peter and Bunny Wailer. I asked if I could take their picture and Bob laughed at my cockney accent and I was equally intrigued by his rude bwoy yard accent. He seemed quite surprised that I was taking pictures. We talked and I was fascinated about what was taking place in JA at the time and he was fascinated by England. Eventually he told me that they had a tour coming up and asked would I like to come along. So I went on the tour. I packed my bags and just disappeared. From there we built up a friendship. I did the tour for a week and then it broke down, because they woke up one morning and it was snowing. They hadn't seen snow before and they thought it was a sign from Jah that they ought to go home. They had an argument about it. Bob stayed. The others went home.

You also have some rare photos of Michael X.

Yes, I knew Michael from being at the Black House. Michael had a funny background. He was an enforcer for Rachman. Rachman was a Jewish landlord. It was difficult for immigrants to get houses to rent at the time. The common sign of the time was 'No blacks, No Irish, No dogs.' Rachman specialised in renting to immigrants. Michael was his enforcer who collected the rent.

Somewhere in the seventies, Michael switched to being England's answer to Malcolm X. He opened the Black House, which was funded by John Lennon of the Beatles. The Black House had a library, entertainment, kitchen, music, and it was a hostel. It was a unique place at the time. But Michael had confused ideas. He was anti-white, but at the same time he surrounded himself with white people. I thought that was weird. Eventually the house closed down and he moved back to Trinidad where he was from. He was later hanged for murder.

Did you experience any obstacles as a black photographer?

I guess the fact that I was the only black photographer around was sometimes an obstacle. People were always surprised because they had never seen a black photographer. But I always made things work for me. I kept pushing and doors eventually opened. I was lucky with the Sex Pistol job because the band were into reggae and they had seen my Bob Marley pictures. Punk and Reggae were the two popular musics at the time. I don't really focus on negativity. As a black photographer you can either disappear or get noticed. I make my colour work for me rather than against me.

I don't let obstacles get in my way. I'm not saying there aren't barriers, but you have to overcome them. It is how you approach it. Skin colour is only a problem if you make it a problem. As a black man I am aware that the first thing people see is my colour and some may hate me for it, but personally I don't let skin colour get in my way. I just get on with my life.

Have you got any recommendations for young photographers starting out?

Get on with it.

How?

Well, the first thing you have to understand if you really love taking pictures it is not easy. It is a competitive career. For every one job there are a hundred photographer chasing it. Make sure it is really what you want to do. There isn't a great deal of money to be made straight away unless you are lucky and get spotted early.

A lot of black kids come up to me and say they want to be

a photographer, but when I speak to them, I find they don't know anything about photography. They just want to do it because of the glamour and they think there is lots of money to be made.

There is more to being a photographer. You have to be able to take knock-backs. When you take pictures and people tell you it's the worst set of pictures they have even seen. How are you going to deal with that? You have to be able to take deep criticism and continue - because you believe in yourself and your ability.

You should know what area of photography you want to go into. Photography is not just fashion and music. There is radiology, the Army, Airforce, the Police, science, weddings. Don't just pursue the glamour. There is good money to be made in all these areas. There is also underwater photography, nature photography, the field is wide open, but remember the equipment is expensive and photography is not always something you can be taught. You can learn the technical side of it, but you need to have a third eye and that can't be taught.

What are you working on at the moment?

I'm still working commercially, and I've done this exhibition. People are discovering my work and by discovering my work, they are discovering a life they have not seen before. I was not commissioned to do this exhibition. In fact, I have lost money. The prints are for sale, but a lot of people won't buy or can't buy. We don't invest in our own art the way other races do. These photos are part of our history and our culture; yet, all our art is owned by white people, because they are the ones who buy it. We are not investing in ourselves.

All our art is gone. People come to my house and they see art and they say, 'Bwoy, you pay for that?' Art is an investment but people would rather buy trainers that fall off their feet in a few months rather than invest in one my photos.

Can I take you back to Jamaica, where you started off? Would you go back there?

I don't see my future in Jamaica. I don't see my future in England either. I could live elsewhere, USA interests me, even Japan or Africa. I don't feel that I belong to any one place. Right now I just want to live my time and do the best I can and make sure that my children get something out of it.

STEPHEN FRY

Stephen Fry is a solicitor living and working in
North London where he runs a joint practice.
He is married with two children.

He recounts his experience of coming to Britain as a
12-year-old, being educated here and working his
way towards his chosen career.

Living the Dream

I did not come with any preconceptions of what Britain would be like. In Grenada we had some impressions of what it was like here from people who had been on holiday, but I deliberately chose to put everything out of my mind and have my own, fresh experience.

My mother had been in Britain for about ten years and I came over with my grandmother to join her and my step-dad. The main problem I had on coming here was adjusting to the climate, but apart from this I found the people and the place mostly quite accommodating. I can't say I had any bad experiences at the time; when I came, it was the late '70s and my mother lived in Tottenham where there were a lot of black people, so I can't recall there being any problems.

When I started school though I had minor a difficulty with the language and other children understanding me. It was more to do with my accent than my inability to speak English, but I consciously tried to change the way I spoke so I could fit in with the other children as quickly as possible. I wasn't being teased as such, it was more curiosity on the other children's part, but I did not like the attention it brought.

One of the first things I noticed about schooling in Britain was that, unlike Grenada, you were placed in a class according to your age and not your ability. So I spent my first year in school going over work I had already done.

By the time I arrived here at age 12, I already knew I wanted to be a solicitor and that has never changed. I was very bright as a child and people in Grenada would say 'you should be a lawyer or a doctor.' As I did not like sciences, law was the natural choice.

At school in Britain I found the teachers very supportive. Race did not come into play as there were a lot of black children in the school. My teacher recognised early on that I had certain abilities, and encouraged me in the right direction. But the grounding was in Grenada. My aunts, uncles and various cousins had been through the system and they constantly reinforced the values of education to me.

I had never wavered from what my family instilled in me, though like most people I succumbed to a certain amount of peer pressure when I was younger. At the age of about 16, I went through the usual phase of hanging out with my friends and other children who were not aiming high in the way I was, but I managed to remain focused and always knew what I wanted to achieve.

As a child I was always quite disciplined and naturally motivated, so I had no intention of being led astray. I left school at 18 with nine 'O' levels and three 'A' levels. I proceeded straight on to do my Law degree without taking any time off. After this, I spent two years doing my pupillage and have been working as a solicitor since then.

Even though I found it relatively easy to get to this stage I realised that law is a very competitive field, and that students coming through now will find it a lot more difficult. I believe I am in a position to help other black people coming up through the profession and have done so for a number of years. I am involved with the 'Afro-Caribbean and Asian Lawyers' group (ACAL). We provide support and assistance to students by helping with CVs, interviews and assist them with gaining training contracts.

In 1988, after completing my Law Society finals, it took me only three months to get a training contract with a firm of solicitors. At the time there was a deficiency of solicitors, so it was a good time to get into the profession. Currently there is a surplus of solicitors, so students are having to wait on average about one year to get a placement. ACAL has been in operation since 1991 and we have managed to help many people to attain their goals.

I also set up TOP (Towards Our Potential), a Saturday school for black children. The premise behind TOP is to help instill educational values in today's children and as the title suggests, help them to achieve their potential. Children today have a lot of influences which makes it difficult to guide them in a proper educational way. They have a lot of distractions that people of my age and older did not have, and usually they have no idea what their parents or grandparents went through.

On the whole I feel black, third generation children have not followed on with the dream of their parents. They feel Britain is their country, and there seems to be no sense of urgency about them doing well; things come their way too easily. I feel the problem with many people born in Britain is that they have not seen anything else, so do not know how good they have it. They have not seen the other side where people are not so fortunate, and can distance themselves. Second generation people, such as myself, strove harder and just about did OK.

I have been working as a solicitor for eight years. The last two years I have been in a partnership where we employ eight staff, including a legal team of three. I personally deal with non-contentious issues such as wills, probates and matters that do not generally go to court. It's impossible to imagine myself doing anything else and so my future aspirations have to be to establish myself as an authority in an area of specialisation. Once you've made your mark and established yourself, for example as an excellent entertainment lawyer, it will obviously help to bring in more clients and maintain the client base one already has.

Our client group at present is very mixed. The firm has been established in the area for 100 years so we have generations of the same families using us as well as small local firms. We do not set out specifically to attract black clients but the mix of the area means that we work with people of different nationalities as well as income brackets.

I have tried to instill the same principles I hold that helped me to succeed into my children and will find out in time whether it has worked. It is up to parents such as myself to educate their children to bring about a change. Black people here are now so diverse with many different interests and views. There's no mass identity as before so it's hard to know in which direction to proceed. However, I am pleased to have come to Britain and to have achieved what I have. Like most people I have thoughts about going back home. It was my intention to do so once I qualified but due to having a young family I did not manage to go. At the back of my mind is still the intention to go home, but the longer you are here, the more difficult it becomes!

CHARLOTTE ENGLISH

Charlotte English came to England from Clarendon, Jamaica in 1964. She is a successful businesswoman and proprietor of the *'Breadfruit Bar'* in Battersea, London. She is also a mother of two grown-up children.

Lost Souls

Tell me about your early life and how you came to Britain.

I came to England at about aged eight to join my mother after
being looked after by several different sets of people in
Jamaica. My mother had abandoned me as a baby and I was
initially taken care of by my grandmother, but she became too
ill to look after me so I was passed around. As no one was
paying these people for my keep, my grandmother arranged
for me to be sent to England to join my mother who was now
married and had three other children.

Unfortunately within a year of arriving in England I was
'abandoned' for a second time by my mother. What actually
happened was that I was being beaten, starved and generally
abused so I was taken into care by social services. I believe
my mother's husband did not want me to be a part of the
family and that is why the abuse took place. I was the only
one treated this way.

**You obviously had a horrendous start in life. How did
this impact on your moving to England and acclimatising
to the culture?**

I loved England. It was cold and very foggy but I just loved
everything about it. I went to school and had school dinners,
loved it and still do. I thought everything was fantastic. The
teachers and children at school were fantastic, and really kind.
I've always had a good time in Britain. Possibly the horrible

way I was treated from birth in Jamaica, and when I came to England to join my mother meant that the wet and damp climate fitted my mood. But I also loved cups of tea, fires, being able to turn a tap on and having a bath. To me this was luxury. Not having to go to fetch water to have a bath was great.

I also did not feel that the British culture was that different to what I was familiar with in Jamaica. In Clarendon there were quite a number of English couples living near to me and I often went to their houses. They were always friendly, so when I arrived in Britain I did not have any problems fitting in. Maybe there was prejudice but coming from Jamaica, where I did not have a family or people who wanted me, I did not miss anything. To me I was simply leaving one place for another. I was just happy that people were friendly and treated me right. I went to a school in Crystal Palace and I do not remember having a bad day there.

In Jamaica teachers at school were like tyrants who would beat you for anything, so as far as I was concerned, in England I was away from all that and that's what mattered.

You have come a long way since. You are now a businesswoman with your own bar/restaurant. How did this process begin?

Firstly I have to say that I have always been really lucky in my life since I've been here. After being taken into care at about nine or ten, I was adopted by a widow at around 13 years old. Her husband had died in the war and her children grown up so I became her new family. The good thing about having this older 'mother' who actually loved and wanted me was that she always told me, 'whatever you want, you can have.' In other words, she was saying that I could achieve what I wanted and that she was there to help me do so if I wanted, or I could do it my own way if I preferred. So I took her message on, if

I needed help I asked for it, otherwise I got on with it, and that's how it's always been. She was always there for me, gave me guidance, and bags of confidence which I still have.

In relation to the business side, I've had restaurants most of my working life. When I left school I studied law, but then I got married and started to raise a family. Having been an abandoned child I wanted to look after my children myself, so I decided to give up law and find a career that would allow me to still work and be a mother. I decided to do a catering course at 'Pru Leith's' in Notting Hill, and from there I started doing foods for bands, and my first restaurant led out of that.

In total, I've had about six different restaurants. Various things have happened to me such as falling ill and divorce, which have meant me not holding on to businesses in the past, but I've had the current one (Breadfruit Bar) for the past two years and I intend to build on this.

What are some of the difficulties you have faced in business?

Acquiring finance can be difficult so that is why I've never looked for it. I just earn the money and do things in stages. I have never borrowed money to get anything going. I earn and pay for it myself. I've also never had or wanted a business partner, and have always managed to get my restaurants going and nurse them along until they come together.

I have had help from really nice people, and I've also come across the ones who will steal and cheat but that is part of life. I just try to stay close to those that I know are good people.

Who is your clientele?

Although we do Caribbean food this is not a Caribbean restaurant. We do a mix of foods, particularly what is known as 'shoot foods'. In other words, we cater for the film and television industry when they are on location shoots, we feed the cast and crew.

In the evenings we will do pre-ordered Caribbean foods, although we rarely have Caribbean customers who actually come into the bar. One of my most loyal Caribbean customers is Neville Lawrence (father of murdered teenager Stephen Lawrence) who brings in both Caribbean and English customers. We mainly have an English and continental clientele and as we don't currently advertise we tend to get known about through word of mouth. Because we work a lot within the film industry, we get known in that circle. I know that there are very few Caribbeans in this circle but I find in general that Caribbeans do not seem to like having their culture on show. They seem to prefer it to be a secret, enjoyed in the confines of their home and so as a result don't want to pay to have it out in the open. They don't realise how important it is to be shown. Caribbean food is absolutely adored by others but Caribbeans need to learn more about culture and how to share while retaining it. Our public culture is usually narrowed down to music and dance.

Is this a reason you think why Caribbean food is not as popular as other ethnic groups?

Partly, but I think a lot of Caribbeans felt that they were pressed into coming here and they never intended to stay so they did not put down any roots. For example, people of my mother's generation in many ways felt they were being kept here against their will so embarking on businesses such as opening a restaurant did not occur to them. You will also find that other cultures such as Asians have their own cultural centres where you can go to experience their food amongst other things, but to my knowledge there's no such place for Caribbeans here.

You can go to places such as Brixton, but it's not a positive reflection of what our culture is. White people go there to observe, cream off the best and package it, while the black people just remain there and exist. They're not in control, own very little of it and are basically pushed around. That's how they know it, and don't want to change it. Black people often say they're fighting for equality but they don't really mean it. It's just a token gesture.

Business is one way many ethnic communities have made their mark in Britain. Do you see this as an avenue that could be exploited by Caribbeans?

Unfortunately I don't, not on any great scale anyway. A lot of Caribbean people in this country could have really good businesses but they don't want to start at the beginning and work their way through. They get an idea and start in the middle. They go to a bank without a business plan, get told to go away and then say it's racism. But they need to understand that in order to build a business there must be a foundation. It doesn't matter if you have no money, what matters is if you have a plan which you've worked through and committed to paper which you can show to anybody and say, 'what do you think of this?' If it's good they'll most probably say 'yes', if there's no plan, you'll get laughed at and that's what happens to a lot of Caribbean people. It means Caribbeans with good plans are often not given the time of day because there are more time wasters than there are practical people, but because we're all seen as black Caribbeans, no one wants to listen. So in the majority of cases it isn't the banks or the government who drags us down, it is ourselves because we won't go from A to B to C but from A to Z, with nothing in between. Africans and Asians seem to make it happen, but Caribbeans as a whole can't see that going from A straight to Z will not work. They don't seem to understand about foundations, which is odd, because most Caribbeans come from farming communities where you have to plant a seed and water it to make it grow, but they have forgotten or lost themselves.

Do you think that many people share your views?

A lot of people won't want to hear what I have to say, although many do think the same as I do but would not voice it for fear of being ostracised. Well, I don't have a lot of black friends (or white ones) but I do know a lot of people and it's an absolute fact that if we don' t face up to these issues then we're a dying breed. We should hear it, recognise it and act on it.

How do things move forward?

There are black people doing really good things. One example is the Labour MP, Diane Abbott who instigated an initiative called 'Black Women Mean Business', which is brilliant. The idea of this is to attend functions, usually held at the House of Commons, where you can meet entrepreneurs such as Richard Branson, various chief executives and negotiate a business deal with them if you have something sound to offer. There are also other middle class black people doing things, but they are rarely heard, they are just in the wilderness.

But the solution is to get on your own and make it work. Forget about any community responsibility. If you meet like-minded people you can have a chat and associate; if you want to work together then do but everyone has to do it for themselves.

Do you think people such as yourself who have done

well have fulfilled some of the dreams Caribbeans came here to achieve?

No, because I don't feel it was right for Caribbeans to have left their countries to go to another country and rebuild it while their own countries have been left unbuilt. The Caribbean has been raped by two or three generations of farmers, engineers and other professionals and what we've contributed to this country in terms of labour has not been recognised. We have no stake here despite all the work put in and our own countries are some sixty years behind. Some small personal dreams have been met but in the overall scheme of things we have not really achieved anything. I only know of one black family who have achieved massive success, that is, untold riches, but nearly all have nothing to show for all their years here. The majority of Caribbeans still live in council housing and have paid rent all their lives, and worked for places such as the railways; as far as I'm concerned that is a waste of a life. Why leave your country for this? Yes, some of us have achieved small successes but this amounts to very little overall.

How do you see the future for your business?

At the moment it is doing very well. I have a helpful bank manager and I'm in the process of opening another two places. We are going to be here for a very long time.

ENID WILLIAMS

Enid Williams came to England in 1962 to join her parents. She was six years old. She grew up in South London. In 1982, aged 24, she decided to return to Jamaica to settle. She married there and had two children. She has recently returned to England after 20 years in Jamaica. We spoke with her about her experience of being a returnee.

Returning; for better or worse

I came to England on Independence day. It was August 6th, 1962 and I remember it well. I was a little annoyed that we were leaving then, because I missed out on all the Independence Day gifts that the other children got at school. I came over with my brother. My father came over in 1960 and my mother in 1961, so as unaccompanied children, we were looked after by the air hostesses. That was my first real contact with white people. I remember they gave me a green egg. Well, it was a boiled egg - but the yolk was green. The green egg stuck in my memory. Now, I always remember that is what happens to an egg after it has been boiled a while.

What were your first impressions of England?

I remember seeing television for the first time. I remember a particular programme, where the man was rolling down a woman's stockings, and my brother who was eleven at the time was paying particular interest. My mother saw his response and banned television immediately. I also remember that our first winter was very bad. There was a lot of snow. It was very scary.

I started at Effra Primary School in Brixton. There was a nice lady teacher and she was trying to help me with my pronunciation. She taught me how to say 'the' instead of 'de' and I got over that little problem successfully. School was great! It was a big school with lots of children. We also had wonderful Christmases with a Christmas tree which we never had in Jamaica. I was six years old so I just got on with life. I suppose it may have been different for my brother who was eleven and close to puberty - so there was a lot going on for him to adjust to.

After growing up in England, you decided to return to Jamaica. What prompted your decision to return and what preparations did you make?

Well, after we left school, my best girlfriend and I decided to go on holiday to Jamaica and we fell in love with the place and the sunshine. It was so hot when we got off the plane. Everything just seemed right. We decided then that sometime in the future we would definitely return for good.

We returned to England after our holiday and we started college, but I think from then on we were always preparing to return in our minds. After college, I went to university and got a degree and then I worked hard and got some money together. I felt with my degree and level of education, I had lots of skills and I would be alright in Jamaica. I felt I had a lot to offer. I didn't make any special preparations. For me it was the romance of going that mattered most to me. You see I left Jamaica as a child and I didn't have any choice about leaving. Now I had a choice. I could go back and do something for my country. Finally, in 1982 at the age of 24, I decided it was time to go. My girlfriend and I made no preparations as to where we were going to stay. At first, we just 'kotch' with family. We could not rent because we didn't have jobs as yet.

It took a while to find work. Unfortunately, for me I had studied French and German at university. French and German were practically useless in Jamaica, so I wasn't as prepared as I should have been. The first place I went to for a job was the Ministry of Foreign Affairs because of my languages, but nothing happened there. Later I got a job as a journalist.

At work I felt that I was different immediately. There was a girl at work who called me Queen Elizabeth - because of my mannerisms. I suppose to them, we were very English. I bought some Tamerind balls in a shop one day and when I got to work I realised that the Tamerind balls were bad. So I told my colleagues that I was going to take them back to the shop. Straight away there were peals of laughter. No one ever takes anything back in Jamaica. You either consume it or throw it away. Anyway, I ignored them and took the sweets back. The shopkeeper was most apologetic and replaced them.

Despite my success the office was convinced I was mad because I had stuck up for my rights. I also remember wearing a skirt to work one day and it was a stripe denim skirt. When I got to work, people were looking at me in a strange way, until one of the girls came up and told me I was wearing the uniform of the Jamaican constabulary. So at work everyone just constantly had a laugh at my expense. I realised I was different. I was the same colour and I thought I would fit in and be comfortable, but I was different.

I worked for an organisation called JAMPRO, which promotes investment into the country and exports out. My job entailed wooing investors. When they came from abroad I took them to all the places and sites they needed to go or wanted to see in order to set up business in Jamaica. I was made redundant from that job because I was too vocal and I did my job properly. There were people there who did not do their job properly but they did not lose their job.

It was also in Jamaica that I felt racism for the first time, much more that I had ever felt it in England. It was in Jamaica I realised what shade of black I was. In England I was just black but in Jamaica you can be red, brown, light, white. I felt the racism from both white and black people. White people in Jamaica are very arrogant and very aggressive. They still carry the mentality of the plantation. They still live in the big houses and the darker skin people are still the slaves. We were outsiders from the moment we got there, even though I went there thinking this was home. But when I arrived, I felt I was in the wrong place. The black people in Jamaica don't like themselves very much, possibly because of the racism and the hierarchy of shadism that is hard to believe. The African population who are 90% of Jamaicans, are treated like second-class citizens by the 10% at the top, who still own everything.

People say I'm too sensitive, but I'm not stupid, I know what I felt.

I don't think being English made any difference to me being treated better. In fact, it was a disadvantage. Everyone in Jamaica thinks that English people are mad. Some people told me to keep my accent, but as a linguist I don't retain accents for long, but I met people who had been there for years and they still had their Queen's English accent.

When we left Jamaica with our parents, we left a country that was civilised at that point. When we return we still think Jamaica is at the point we left it. We don't realise it has changed a lot. England is not in vogue anymore, everyone is influenced by America now. The young in particular look to America, whereas the old still look to mother England. The young who go to America, always maintain contact with Jamaica and return frequently, unlike those of us who came to England, stayed away for 20 to 30 years before going back. This makes it harder to go back and for us to be accepted.

What made you stay in Jamaica, despite all the problems you encountered?

Well my girlfriend left after a couple of years, she wanted to come back to England to further her education. I may have left at the same time as her, but I met my future husband - so at that time our paths went in different directions. She came back and I stayed on. I just dealt with the problems and got on with my life.

Thinking back now I may have left England prematurely at

24, because having done a first degree, I had no profession as such, particularly one that would have been useful in Jamaica. As I said, I had done French and German at university, which is not relevant to Jamaica, so I should have prepared myself better.

Anyway, I got married and I just settled into the rhythm of life. My husband and I bought a house, we had two children and soon one just forgot about England. Also, my mother, father and brother came back to Jamaica. My parents always wanted to return and they were overjoyed that we were all there together. With my family around me, I did not have to think of England anymore. Also, if I wanted anything like consumer items, which I missed from England - it was easy to fly to Miami - which we did frequently, so I did not miss anything.

My husband is a lawyer, and financially we had a good existence. The children started at a private school, which my husband insisted on - so our future was secured.

How did you feel about your children going to school in Jamaica?

I had no problem with my children growing up in Jamaica and going to school there. The education system in Jamaica is very good, particularly if you go private. The system is perhaps a little archaic, but it prepares children for the society they live in. For example the curriculum deals with the Americas and Caribbean. The education is very positive. The private schools and church schools are very good. Everybody wants to get into them. Although I think the ordinary schools are very poor in resources and staff, a lot of them are struggling. I suppose as well it is easier for a child going to school in Jamaica, because there are lots of black professional role models around for them to see and aspire towards. In England the education system can mitigate against black children, particularly if you are not positive and you don't know what is achievable.

So you are back in England now. After 20 years in Jamaica, what made you come back?

I was apprehensive about coming back, especially as the children were happy growing up in Jamaica and didn't want to come. Also, I had to leave my husband behind; he is currently studying for the English bar exams, so he can practice in England.

I came back because I just got tired of Jamaica. I got tired of the arrogance, the potholes, the power cuts, the water shortage and the way the society just seems to be going down and the blatant corruption, especially in high places. I felt sad for Jamaica. I felt sad because we were not moving forward and everyone is aware of why - it's because of the politicians and yet people put them on a pedestal. The other day before I left, they had bought in a tax similar to VAT and it turns out that two ministers at the top owed millions in this tax. How can a country move forward when those in charge are blatantly corrupt? I just got impatient with what was going on back home. One reason I went to Jamaica, I remind myself, was to make a difference. After twenty years, I can't see that I have made a difference. Jamaica is going backwards.

On top of everything they stole my car. That was the last straw. When I reported my car stolen, the policeman who came said I was lucky I wasn't in it, because they would have killed me. So I just packed up my children and left.

Jamaica has tremendous potential but the wrong people are in power. The people in power cannot see a future for the island. They are selfish and they are very short-sighted. They just see a future for themselves. They want the prominence and financial gain of their position , but it is the people who are suffering. Furthermore, they fuel the violence every time there is an election. Guns flood into the country and the poor people kill each other over politics and politicians who are not helping them.

I look at the whole situation and I can see that if someone was running the country properly, things could be achieved.

I got really depressed and frustrated because this was my country and I couldn't do anything to help. I went to Jamaica to make a difference, unfortunately I didn't or couldn't or wasn't allowed to. At the end of the day Jamaicans are quite happy doing things their way and they don't really want to change and perhaps it is arrogant of us to think we can go there and make change, whether people want it or not.

So what recommendations would you make to someone who wants to return?

I would say there is no utopia anywhere. I wouldn't stop anyone from going to Jamaica. In fact, I intend to send my children home on regular visits, so they don't lose contact with their country and culture. Ideally, I would like them to spend six months in England and six months in Jamaica, so they will feel equally at home in both countries. If they eventually decide to settle in Jamaica, I hope it will not be a huge adjustment for them as it was for me.

I would recommend Jamaica to anyone who wants to return. I think they should go, but don't go with false hopes, go with your eyes wide open. Remember that Jamaica has changed a lot. It is not the Jamaica you left 20 or 30 years ago and it has lost a lot of its altruism. The older generation of returnees are very trusting and become easy prey. So, you won't necessarily change the society, in fact the society will change you, but be flexible and don't go with fixed ideas. Above all, what is required is a very open mind.

GEORGE KELLY

George Kelly was born in 1943 in Kingston, Jamaica. He is a sculptor and he lives in London with his family.

Fokowan: A Lone Journey To Success

I lived in Jamaica until the age of fourteen, when I came to England to join my parents. Growing up in Jamaica in the 1940s and '50s we did not have a lot but we were happier without the abundance people are used to today. From an early age I loved working with my hands. I can remember as a small boy making my own toys. For example I would get hold of a six-inch nail and beat it with a heavy stone until it was flat, then I would sharpen it and use it as a knife or a chisel or a screwdriver.

At the age of four I started elementary school. This was the East Queen Street Baptist Elementary School that was attached to the church. My life in Jamaica was a happy and contented one and I did not see any reason to leave - but if I had to leave I would have preferred to go to America. A lot of our ideas about different places at that time came from the cinema and comic books. I was a cinema lover and I loved American movies more than any other, in particular I loved cowboy and gangster movies. To me America was far more exciting than England. The memories of England that English movies left me back then were of Sherlock Holmes, Jack the Ripper and foggy cobbled stone streets. It was not a place I was attracted to - but my parents chose to come to England. My father left Jamaica first in 1955, followed by my mother a year later, then I came in 1957 with my younger brother, who was aged seven at the time.

Do you remember the journey to England and what were your first impressions?

We came on an aeroplane, which was unusual at the time as then most people travelled by ship. I remember that the plane we came on was very rickety and so we had to stop for two days and nights in New Jersey, USA while it was repaired. This was a first hand experience of the America I had seen in the movies. It seemed larger than life and very, very exciting.

We eventually arrived in England on the 12th September at the beginning of autumn. There was an emotional reunion with our parents and a drive in a taxi to Brixton. The first place I lived was 3 Geneva Road SW9 in a house that was 4-5 storeys high. To me it did not look like a house but a multi-storey dungeon. It was a multiple occupation tenement, with about thirty people yet it had only one toilet. My father had rented a double bed from the landlord for himself, my brother and I in a large room on the top floor. There were three other occupied single beds. I can still remember the cardboard suitcases, on top of the wardrobes and the greasy gas cooker on the landing where everyone cooked their meals. My mother and her friend occupied a room two floors below. The toilet was situated in the basement and it seemed to me no one ever cleaned it. It had no window and the door could not be locked. From the sunshine, outdoor life I'd led before, this was like coming into a nightmare. Back home I had my own bedroom and took a shower every morning before going to school. Here there wasn't even a bathroom. We had to go to the public baths at Camberwell Green once every fortnight and that was the only time we washed our whole body. I was very unhappy for the first six months until my parents were able to get a flat for the family.

I started school and spent two years there trying to make sense of my new environment and the people. The two years

I spent at school here were a rather strange experience. I went to Kennington Secondary Modern Boys School and out of around 500 pupils, there were only five of us black boys. Of course I was picked on regularly, and so I had to learn to defend myself.

The first time I saw snow I was very excited. My classmates and I had a snowball fight that morning at school and my hands got very cold. I decided I did not like snow and would not touch it again. By the end of the first week the snow had turned into granules of ice. I remember being in the schoolyard one afternoon when it dawned on me that I was the only person standing on one side of the yard. Suddenly lumps of ice granules started coming my way - dozens of them it seemed. I rushed out of the schoolyard to a building site across the road where there were lots of broken bricks and concrete laying around, which I picked up and put in my pockets. I went back into the schoolyard and of course the ice balls started coming towards me again; I rushed at the boys who were throwing the ice balls, flinging pieces of bricks and concrete like a mad man. That surprised them and they fled for cover. Later some of them came up to me and asked me what was wrong. I told them that I wasn't into playing with ice balls because where I came from we fling bricks and stones not ice. After that I had no more problems in the school. To me that was the beginning of the long process of understanding white people; I've spent the last 43 years of my life preoccupied with that.

How did you develop your interest in sculpting?

Well that is a long story. I did not start sculpting until I was in my thirties.

When I left school I started work as an apprentice projectionist at the local cinema in Brixton, I later worked at various clerical jobs ending up as a postman. During that time

I also developed an interest in music. I taught myself to play the flute and the conga drums. After struggling with the instruments for a while making strange and foul sounds I woke up one morning to find that I could make music. I realised then that I could master anything through my own endeavours, if I applied myself with perseverance and patience. That was a turning point in my life, it became a paradigm for my life.

Music gave me the opportunity to travel to America with a band called Cymande which did quite well with a record called The Message. Later someone introduced me to Jimmy Cliff and I travelled with him as a sound engineer to Nigeria. My visit to Nigeria was a real, life-transforming experience. To begin with, it was just like Kingston in many ways, yet different, except it was more like Kingston than Kingston. I mean the people were blacker, they had the same kind of vitality, only they were more vital. There was a kind of mystery about them that I'd never encountered before. I knew the people, I recognised in them my parents, my cousins, my grandfather, and the people who lived next door back home in Jamaica. I saw them all there, and more. By then I'd been in England for some years and so had gotten out of the habit of seeing large numbers of black people. That visit to Nigeria was the beginning of my journey into facing the reality of being black living in a white dominated world.

Your music career appears to have been quite successful so why did you not continue on that path?

Although the bands I'd played with did pretty well and I had travelled and worked with a famous singer, I never really saw myself as a professional musician. I have always been a person with many interests and through music I realised that I could become proficient at anything I chose to do. However, what made me change direction was my visit to the ancient city of

Benin in Nigeria. This was the place where in pre-colonial times some of the greatest works of art ever created was produced. The first sight of this art I believe transformed my life, for it was the first time I had seen black people depicted as great kings and queens and noble warriors.

Jimmy Cliff had a gig at a football stadium in that place, and while setting up the p.a. system a young man approached me looking for work. I swear he was the spitting image of a piece of African carving - a sculpture. He was about six feet tall with fine-boned limbs and a flat forehead. His image has remained with me ever since. I realised then what the African carvers all try to do, that is to capture in their art the essence of the tribe, the archetypal first being that represents the soul of the group. Another strong image that has stayed with me is that of an old man sitting under a tree. He looked like something from the beginning of time; drenched in wisdom and knowledge of the things I was struggling to make sense of about myself and Africa. I knew that this old man had something important to tell me, something I would not find in any European institution. He had sent word for me to come and see him but I was too busy with my work to spend a few minutes with him, something I have regretted ever since.

I returned to England deciding that I wasn't going to do music anymore because of the spirit and the feelings I got from my visit to Benin. I was now seeing rather than hearing. I decided I would set about applying the same method I used to learn music to the visual arts. I slowly developed my own way of creating sculptures.

I started sculpting seriously around 1980. It began with a dream I had one night about materials I could use to make sculpture and so I got up next morning and went out and bought a bag of plaster and some carving tools.

A lot of what I do, as a sculptor is around trying to recapture the feelings those two people evoked in me back there in

Nigeria in 1974, and of course what that old man sitting under the tree had to say to me. My art has become a search for that knowledge that had to be deferred.

How did you develop your craft? Were you self-taught or did you go to art school?

I did not feel the need to go to any school of art because I was in my early thirties, and was quite mature politically and philosophically. You see, I had been an avid reader since leaving school at sixteen. I read everything I could get my hands on; philosophy, religion, psychology, politics, everything. Sometimes my friends would not see me for days when I would lock myself away and just read. All the reading I had done to that point had one thing in common, that was that there was nothing positive in Africa. Africa had contributed nothing to world civilization. My visit to Nigeria changed all that of course. I therefore decided I could not go to the same white people who wrote those books for them to teach me about African art and philosophy. In this world in which we live, if the great white master does not validate success, it has no value so I have set myself the task of proving that there are other paths to success other than the one presided over by the great white master. Therefore, I had to find ways of penetrating and accessing information and knowledge about Africa and myself without subjecting myself to them. I decided then that sculpting would be a long, lonely journey. Having gained a sense of the philosophy of what one wanted to express all that remained was the unravelling of the technical aspects, which of course is achieved through trial and error. After many years for struggle to perfect my craft, I eventually produced a piece that I felt was close enough to an ideal. I was then ready to confirm my transformation into an artist; I chose the name

Ona Fowokan, which is Yoruba for the artist who creates with the hand.

Eventually I arrived at a more balanced view of things African and a better sense of the notion of Africa that I wanted to depict in my art. The two men I encountered in Nigeria have become my archetypes. Their essence or spirit appears in everything I have created, whether male or female. My life's work I believe is to continue the journey into the mystery that those two beings represent.

Who do you create your work for - your main audience?

I create my work primarily for black people because I think we have been through a very debilitating history over the past four hundred years which has turned us into a parody of something we can never be. We can only be like white people we can never be white people. The world in which we live, however, is the product of the white man's psyche rather than our own. Yet we are expected to live and compete on equal terms with them. I know I can never be equal to, or beat them at their own games - they set the pace and make the rules at all times, that is why I felt it necessary to find an African path.

The irony though is that most black people have difficulty dealing with the art the black artists produce. For most of us art in our homes was usually a picture of the last supper or the image of a crucified white Christ upon a cross. When I first started showing my work it was a real struggle getting them to even look at my work. I was often accused of dealing in voo-doo and black magic. Yet, those same black people would find the work acceptable if white people showed an interest in it. Things have changed a lot since, black people are a lot more comfortable seeing themselves depicted in art - so now the next step is for them to start looking beyond the image to the meaning that lies behind. Of course I know this is not going to be easy. Europeans have had a long tradition of collecting art. But for us traditionally art was a part of our environment, of our everyday life. It was central to religion and ritual, and not just something decorative that is placed on the wall. We have not yet made the transition to art for art sake.

Take for example that piece over there on the wall; it is from the Ivory Coast. Now most of the people who see it are frightened of it. Their first reaction when they see it is to associate it with voodoo or black magic. Yet all it is, is a ritual mask relating to male circumcision. If you look at it you will see that it is a mixture of human and animal. It has a human face, the horns of antelope and the trunk and tusks of an elephant. The first thing most people see however are the horns of a goat, and of course straight away they associate it with something negative; the horns of the goat is a symbol of evil in Western religion and mythology. However as you can see, this piece is not frightening at all. It is an expression from the African psyche. What it tells us is that in life one should strive to be as powerful as the elephant and as fleeting as the antelope.

Your portraits are very life-like. How do you achieve this?

Well, I'm not really conscious of the process. I just know that if I persevere long enough I eventually arrive at an image, which satisfies a vision within me. There is an expression of vitality in my sculptures that people describe as spiritual. There is no orthodox theoretical base to the way I work. I don't use instruments to measure for example. I arrive at an end product through a process of intuition, which you could describe as inner vision, which I believe comes from working within an African world view. The images I create express a quality of spirituality, which I find lacking in Western art. I find their

sculptures totally spiritless and devoid of life; I don't know if
that is deliberate.

I really like the piece 'Meditation Beneath Duppycherry Tree'.

This piece deals with the notion of metamorphosis. It is
made of iron resin; which is a kind of plastic mixed with
powdered iron. It was buried in the soil around the time I lost
my mother. Some months later I dug it up and noticed it had
taken on a rusty, aged appearance. The rust gives it a peculiar
quality of life. I belief in the ancient African concept of infinity,
where life gives birth to life and even death gives birth to life.
It is female because for me the female form is the embodiment
of spiritual power. The 'duppy' is a benevolent spirit in Jamaica.
It also reminds me of my first morning at school when I sat in
my class beneath a duppycherry tree in tears because I was
missing the security of my mother and home. This piece brings
back a lot of memories of my early childhood in Jamaica.

Is it possible to make a living from you work as an artist?

I barely scratch a living, and in order to do so I have to create
pieces that are strictly commercial. This enables me to create
other works that for me are the real purpose of my gift. Those
pieces I will never sell.

One of the dilemmas that haunts me is that most of the
work I produce is bought by white people. You make the work
for your community and they are not really interested in it and
so you have to sell it to those who are willing to buy. I try to
explain the need for these objects in our community, that they
are for our grandchildren, but the reality is that our grandchildren
may never see them. For example last year I sold four pieces
at the Royal Academy of Art Summer Show. They were

delivered to white, middle class suburban homes where black people will never enter. Those pieces are now totally lost to our community - maybe years from now they will end up in museums and art galleries, but how many black people visit museums and art galleries? Our people do not yet appreciate the need for culture and how culture is created through accumulation. Culture is the accumulation of, not just material wealth but of our intellectual and spiritual achievements as well. We will continue to be a deprived people with no culture at all of our own. We have been through slavery and colonialism, periods in which we were not allowed to accumulate materially, spiritually or intellectually; whatever we produced was taken away to be accumulated somewhere else, now we have to start again from scratch. If black people do not accumulate they will never progress, for without culture there can be no progress. We will continue to be a race of consumers of other people's achievements.

The community must begin to appreciate and support the creative talents it has. The artists, writers, philosophers etc. for they are the ones who have the ability to reflect our true inner aspirations. Hopefully in the future, the pieces I have reserved from sale will remain in our community and there will be institutions in which our people will be able to see and enjoy them.

Can you describe your working environment?

I work in a shed at the top of my garden, which is on a hill. Because it is small I am forced to work in a modular way. The space is limiting but it is close to nature. Sometimes I go there on a really cold winter morning to find the clay I'm modelling completely frozen. In the summer by midday it is boiling so I have to get out and work outdoors. However, I enjoy being up there because of its closeness to nature. I am able to keep in touch with the seasons and the wild life as they go through their changes.

That shed reminds me of the times I spent in my grandfather's shack in the slums of West Kingston when I was a young child. It had a rather crude bed and the walls were covered with magazine and newspaper cuttings. Underneath his bed however, were boxes full of books. My grandfather was the only person in my family I ever saw with a book other than the bible. He was a reader and a traveller. He had travelled to Cuba, Panama and the USA and seemed to me to have had all the answers to all the questions. His roof would leak and when it rained everything would be drenched - that's exactly how my shed is and in a way I think I'm still trying to emulate him.

What are you working on at the moment?

At the moment I am working on three pieces to enter for this year's summer show at the Royal Academy of Art. I am also preparing a piece to enter in the Association of Portrait Sculptors' annual exhibition. I've reached a point where there are not a lot of avenues left for me because I insist on retaining control over my work.

Do you have a statement that would sum up your thoughts on art?

Yes. Art is for me is a quest for answers to the following:
Is there a role for art in the traditional sense in our lives today? Is there a need for magic and rituals that mediate between what we have lost and what we have become? Is the purpose of contemporary art to intercede between, us and the forces of civilisation?

How do you see the future?

For me the future and the present are locked up in events in the past. I will continue to strive as I have for the past twenty years or so to express what I believe are the ideals of my community. I am duty-bound to do that. The future in terms of where I will die. I suspect it will be here in England - because my father and mother are buried in the soil of this country and so here is where my bones will lie. I believe that death is the sacred food of rebirth, in it lies purification and renewal; and so we must not forget that it is our deeds and bones that nourish the soil and make the land ours.

ANNETTE SYLVESTER

Annette came to England in 1972 to join her parents.
She is a Community Worker and Photographer.
She lives in London.

The Meaning of the Journey

I was brought up in Grenada by my grandmother. I was brought up with my two cousins. Altogether over fifteen children were brought up in that same house at different times by my grandmother, and gradually they all left as their parents sent for them to go to America, or England. I remember being at school and people asking me if my cousins were my brother and sister, because we lived in the same house. When I was young I did think of them as my brother and sister - it was only when I got older that I began to relate to them as my cousins. I was the youngest of the three children in my grandmother's house, so you could say I was spoilt as I always got away with a lot. I had a great deal of freedom and could go places where my cousins were not allowed. I was always rude to them because I knew they couldn't touch me. I think I was too much for them and often suffered the consequence of my bad behaviour towards them, when they had to look after me. They later left to join their parents in England and I was quite pleased with that because I had the house and my grandmother to myself.

What do you remember about your parents and them leaving?

I remember my mother quite well. I was nearly six when she left. I remember that she was liked by everyone. I remember that she was always sewing my clothes. She was very caring and affectionate towards me. I don't think there has ever been a bad experience between us in my lifetime except the shock of her leaving me. I went to bed one evening and when I woke up next morning she wasn't there. I remember they always talked about her leaving, but because I was a child they did not tell me the actual moment she would leave. I suppose they thought it was best, to save me hurting or crying. Also, I had a substitute mother, my grandmother who took her place easily, and even before she left I was close to my grandmother. But, I held a deep grudge against her for leaving me and I have held it well into my adult life.

My father left when my mother was a few months pregnant with me, but I have always really cared for him. Everyone told me about this wonderful man and I liked him even before I saw him. I was ten when I met him in London for the first time. Up until then I had only seen pictures of him and it was true what everyone said about him, he was a great person. I know it sounds like the typical - blame the mother - psychology. When we talk about the break-up of the family it is always the woman who gets the blame - but it was the way my mother left, that bothered me. The love and care I had was suddenly gone and I resented it.

My mother wrote often and talked about my dad, what they were doing, and where they were living. My grandmother would get someone to read the letters to us. She would send clothes she had sewn for me on my birthday and at Christmas time. They talked about me joining them.

How did you react to the news that you were going to be leaving Grenada for England?

The full implication of leaving did not hit me until a day or two before. I remember I walked everywhere thinking this is the last time I'm going to walk this way. I went to see my friend and I thought this is the last time I'm going to see her. I crossed the river to see my aunty and said it was the last time I'm going to cross this river. It was a childish thing to do but I was mapping everything in my head so that I would remember. Even though it was the last time, I did not want to forget these paths. I could walk them with my eyes closed. In my head I was telling myself that one day I would come back and pass these exact spots, so that was why it was important that I did not forget.

Still, I was glad to come to England. My grandmother didn't want me to stay anymore because she was getting old and couldn't look after me anymore. I felt as if she was rejecting me, but the truth was I was growing into a young woman; which really meant that she did not want me to go through puberty in Grenada. She believed that once children reached puberty they were harder to control and because I was a girl there was the added worry about getting pregnant. I also realised I was no longer a child or her pet and was ready to move on. My grandmother was trying to find someone for me to travel with but she couldn't, so I told her I could go by myself. I thought it was a big adventure.

I came to England in 1972. I was dying to see my father whom I did not know. I recognised my family and they recognised me. They lived in Camden at the time and still do. We had a flat in a house. It was a loft. The ceiling was low. I had to share a bedroom with my brother. He was born here in England. There was a lot of rivalry between us, even though he was only three - but I'd come and taken some space from him so he got jealous.

My father was very fond of me and gave me a lot of attention. I remember that he came to all the school meetings but not my mother. She was a bit cold towards me and saved most of her affection for my brother. She worked quite long hours as a domestic in the city. My father was a tailor back home - but he worked at Fords. Later on he worked in the rag trade in East London. He still does private tailoring and alterations for a big business in Kensington.

So what was it like adjusting to your new environment?

I started primary school and even though it was only for a few months I still had a lot of problems adjusting and fitting in. It was the first place I mixed with other children. I didn't get on too well with the children because they had already formed their groups and found it difficult to let a newcomer in.

There were quite a lot of black children in my school, but even amongst them I stuck out like a sore thumb because I was foreign - but I was quite mouthy and I could stick up for myself. I was always squaring up to the white boys because they were forever being racist. The teachers didn't do anything about it. I was always in front of the head. If I was in school now I'd be excluded - but since I had just come over, they just put it down to having problems settling in.

I was quite good at reading, writing and maths for my age, which is normal for black children to do well in the early schooling but then things change at secondary school. That's how it was for me.

My parents didn't know about the streaming system. They put me in the wrong stream - the bottom stream. I was an embarrassment to the teachers because I shone through and at times I was more or less teaching the class. I would finish my work quickly, get them right and start playing up. So they put me one up - but that was not enough to test me. The school blatantly refused to recognise that I was a bright child - being educated well below my abilities. I only realised something was wrong when another student came who was placed in the bottom stream and she told me she did not want to be there. I asked her why and she explained the streaming system to me and I remember going to the head with her, to make her case. She was such a brilliant student and we became instant friends. You had to be in the right stream to do 'O' levels she told me and she wanted to do 'O' levels. After that I realised what education meant in this country. It was too late for me to achieve anything so I left to go to college to do my 'O' levels.

I think there was a policy at the time, particularly if you came from the Caribbean, that regardless of how educated you were, they would put you in the bottom streams. Our parents had the same problems, as many came here with professional qualifications but could not get work had to settle for unskilled work and labouring.

Yes, and it took us, the victims, to understand the whole situation to be able to change it. Unfortunately, I think a lot of our experience in school was also due to lack of understanding on the part of our parents. I remember my parents persuading me to stay on at school, because the teachers had told them it would look better on my CV and I could get a good reference from the school. However, I knew that the school only wanted me to stay on to bump up their sixth form quota. After that I never gave anyone a chance to tell me what I could or couldn't do and they tried. Even at college I remember one of the teachers asking me why I wanted to study and I told him I wanted to better my grade. He said what makes you think you can do 'A' levels? So I said to him because I got grade Bs in my 'O' levels. Then he told me that 'A' levels were hard.

Even though our parents didn't know a lot about the system they went along with it, because they believed in it. They often met with patronising teachers, who convinced them they knew what was best for their children.

Teachers were always telling you, you've got plenty of time to study. You're still young they use to say - you can afford to spend a year doing nothing - wasting your time. It's a quicker process for white, middle class students. They get their 'A' levels, at eighteen they are at university and at twenty one they finish university and go straight into their first job, and shortly after they climb the promotion ladder.

. . . Whereas for us it is more of an obstacle race and we never get to the finishing line.

It's important for students to be able to live out their potential. It makes you lose interest along the way if you are delayed. If I can't get my way I stop. I change direction, institutions, courses, and therefore I never finish.

So what career did you have in mind when you were at school?

My brother in Grenada is a teacher and I thought about training to be a teacher. I also looked into nursing. The careers advisor didn't know what to make of me. I said I wanted to study. She did not know what to say. She asked all the children what our parents did. I told her my mother was a domestic and my father a tailor. She said, wouldn't I rather do something like that. I said if I studied, I wouldn't want to do those jobs. You don't need qualifications to do those types of jobs. My parents expected me to be a person with qualifications and a career.

It seems as if the teachers and career officers were in collusion - turning out children who followed their parents' footsteps.

That kind of system works in a society where people are controlled but I have a mind of my own. I have rejected the eurocentric curriculum. I don't want to learn about other people in a way that negates myself - the black spiritual self. This kind of teaching is destructive to black children. The only place I could study and be happy would be in Africa or the Caribbean.

I don't think white people realised that black people coming here had high hopes and expectations for their children. They might have been working on the buses but they certainly didn't want their children to do that. I think they expected us to slot in somewhere below the working class. It must have been quite a shock for them to know that we came to do better.

I asked my dad to teach me tailoring and he wouldn't show me because he didn't want me to do it. He did not want me to even think about it, even though tailoring is not such a bad trade.

You've talked about studying within the eurocentric system - but what about working within the system?

I went in the direction of community work. I did a two year certificate in Youth and Community work. On the course there was a lot of talking about situations, but not enough concrete ideas about how to address them.

In work, I find the workers make people depend on them. The society makes people depend on them. No one wants anybody to be empowered. The problem with this way of working is that my ideas come into conflict with my co-workers. I don't want to feel that I'm responsible for keeping things the way they are. I believe in change and that's where the conflict starts. This society has a low opinion of everybody who has not 'made it'. I'm not into education for a piece of paper - I believe in the type of education that people can make use of in their life. I'm into empowerment. My methods work. I reach an understanding with people. I make them see I am approachable. I am open. I make them realise there is a lot they can do. It's mainly communication. It doesn't need more than that. I find that I get a lot of results, mainly by explaining and expressing myself and keeping clear boundaries. Most of the people I worked with are viewed as sick people, even if it's simply a problem with their housing, they are viewed as not well.

I work in hostels and when people come to you for help they already feel that they are less equal to you. If you keep reinforcing that it only means that you are widening the gap between yourself and them. If you close the gap and maintain the respect between you, I find you get better results and you get a better working day.

I'd like to get out of the caring field some day because I've seen what it does to the workers and the people being cared for. You're not wanted in the system and as a black person I understand that very well. For example I never get permanent contracts because there is a part of me that makes it difficult for me to hold back my views. People feel threatened by my confidence and the fact that I am verbal.

They probably think I'm rich and don't need a job - but I do. Someone told me to always keep quiet until my probation is over but I told him I'd be dead by then. I'd be coming into the hostel as one of the clients. I think it's better to speak up. Most jobs I go into I have to tell them about the way they treat me, if they treat me bad. I know my rights and I take them to the union if I have to. I'm always fighting for my rights and most of the time I find myself only doing temporary work because that is what's available to me. Also, sometimes that is all I can handle - to come and go. It's manageable because I don't see the same people and I don't have to put up with the politics and games people play at work. I suppose I can do things that way because I don't rely on that organisation for anything. It's not my sole career. I am always working on the other parts of my life. I have other agendas.

I am into creativity. To add balance to my life I do artistic things such as photography. I am also involved in doing research and taking ideas from the Caribbean culture and finding a way to link them with the culture here in a way that will help people find and strengthen their identity. I am going to document different places that I have travelled to; the history and culture and build up an exhibition. This is all part of my long-term plan to become self-employed. There is a need in this country to empower ourselves, for our own good. Instead of going to work and always trying to educate the boss or your work colleagues - I thought, why don't I just do it as a job and get paid for it? We do so many things for free. We always do more than our share of work anyway and get paid less.

You mentioned mental health earlier - could you talk a bit more about your experience in this area, as so many of our people suffer in that way.

The reason I chose to work in the area of care and documenting our identity through travel is because once your identity is gone, you stop caring and your mental health suffers.

We have forgotten many things that were very important to us. Things to do with our diet for example. Our parents forgot to pass things down to us, because in Britain it is easier to live the western lifestyle. Our diet has changed, which has a bearing on our health, physically and mentally. Unless we take stock of what's happening things will get worse. Mental illness is the result of most of our actions being misdiagnosed. Most of the studies were done a long time ago. Even the medication we take, a lot of it wasn't tested on us. So, we are in fact getting second rate treatment. That's one of the areas I would like to do some research on, to bring it out in the open. I would like to show people how it happens. How from the past you can be traumatised and how the society you live in reinforces that. A lot of the time what we are really suffering from is racism - not mental illness but when we talk about racism we are always told we moan too much and have a chip on our shoulder - and so we shut up, and go mad.

A friend of mine presented herself as mentally depressed and the first thing they did was take her in - since then she has been going through the mental health system. The pressure to succeed as a black person means that you have to be ten times as good to get anywhere and the pressure of racism all lead to anxiety, and of course the more you succeed and study the more aware you become of injustice and racism and that can lead to depression. It's increasing amongst young black people because of the alienation from the society.

A lot of young people are losing their connection to their culture and identity. Some are brought up in care, or have left their parental home. They know they can stay in hostels and their social worker will take care of them. A lot of them find that preferable than putting up with a nagging or strict parent - but they don't always think about the consequences - of being out there in the white structure, until they meet rejection and cannot cope.

You'd be surprised how soon they learn that system. A friend of mine brought her child from Jamaica at a late age recently and she soon learnt the ropes - she left home because her mother dare to hit her. Now, I'm not saying you should abuse a child, but that kind of chastising is normal within Caribbean homes. The child was taken into care and whilst there she became pregnant. They tried to send her back to her mother but by then she was uncontrollable.

You really do have to know yourself in this society. Spend time on yourself outside of work, spend time on therapy that benefits you. Get supervision from people outside of work, don't stay inside the organisation, if the organisation is your problem. Take advice from friends, join black groups or women's group where you can air your views. I never take advice from my boss or supervisor. Why should I? I know my job. It's not very taxing. I know my colleagues' job. I know my boss's job - but unfortunately this society penalise me for knowing too much, rather than reward me.

You have travelled a lot, and earlier on mentioned that your love of travelling and the inspiration probably came from the fact that you travelled at a young age.

I think it is important to travel and live elsewhere. I have spent eighteen months outside of England since I've been here. Travelling means a lot to me. I have thoughts and travelling test them or conclude them. Being in this country you become alienated and forget things, so I can't settle here. For me travelling to other countries where black people are gives me strength. Also, it shows me practices that we possess as a people that are not being shared within the general community anymore. This is a capitalist society that we are living in - everything is for sale, but I would freely share information with people, even if it means it doesn't sell - which doesn't make me a good business person but that doesn't bother me. When I see a better way of life it is so exciting, it adds to my happiness and that is something I want to share.

I went to the country area of Grenada. Some of them couldn't believe it that I came back and fitted in. I did some buying and selling and this allowed me to make contact with a lot of people and they shared what they knew with me. The area of buying fresh food and living off the land appeals to me. The things you think are so important when you are living in a city become unimportant in these countries and you look at

other people in a different way. Their skills matter. In this
country we are alienated as black people but when you go
there and you see a majority of black people getting on in a
particular way it makes you feel at home. Travelling makes
you see things in the opposite way. There are times when
those people need things such as money but they don't sell
their ideas to you, they share them. Here, all we think about is
money.

You went to Africa. What was that like?

You know, my father had told me when I was younger that we
were all Africans. He said that we were all from one continent
and we got spread through slavery. I always thought growing
up that I was a Carib or Arawak and I didn't know which -
because they were the people who first lived on the Islands,
so I thought I must be descended from them but it wasn't until
I first came to this country and I saw all the different types of
black people that I understood what my father meant. That's
why it was important to go to Africa and I remembered what
my father said. I wasn't sure what Africa was before I went.

I went to Zimbabwe and the Gambia in Africa. The shock
I had. I didn't think I would be shocked about Africa, but we
were in Harare, the city, and I thought I would feel at home
but I didn't because the buildings were so large. All I could
see below were the women who came from the country to go
to the market. They were dressed traditionally and some of
them were carrying their baskets on their heads. You see those
big buildings and then you see these little people going to market.
That more than anything represented the inequality. The country
had changed but not enough for the ordinary people. The people
looked very small and that freaked me out.

When I spoke to people I got another shock because they
saw me as different and that was when I realised how divided

we are. The fact that we have different nationalities, different beliefs, speak different languages, placed us on different paths. I was born in the Caribbean and have a British passport which means that I am different even before I open my mouth. Of course it made me realise how much I had changed since leaving Grenada. I also had to realise that there were things in England that I'd gained just by being here. Africa brought all that home and I was in shock for a few days and never got over it till I went to the countryside.

I'm not a city person. I feel out of place in the city. I always head for the country, to the villages and that settles me down quickly. So we were able to see how people actually lived. We got to know the local people in the rural areas. I didn't find their way of life much different from the way I'd grown up in Grenada.

Do you feel that you are still searching for a place or have you found it?

Yes I am still searching and yes I have found a few places that might fit the bill.

What would you say were some of the things you gained and lost as a result of coming from Grenada to England?

The gain is meeting so many different types of our race and linking up with so many different people. I would not have done that if I'd stayed in Grenada. I would not have had the resources to travel as I do. I gained another base, this country. Everything you want to know in this country is in a book so there is a good knowledge base, but nothing can replace what I have lost. I've lost the use of a language which is different and friendships I had made when I was younger. I lost the education. I lost events that happened along the way. When I

went to Zimbabwe they were celebrating heroes' day and I
noticed they had various ceremonies to celebrate which was
important to their life and their culture. In Grenada we had a
revolution and I wasn't there. When it was invaded by the
USA I went on a march to the embassy but it's not the same
as being there.

But all this has happened and I can't change the past. I
have to accept that every generation looks to develop and
improve themselves, which my parents did. They wanted to
improve their conditions and it's only as an adult you see these
things.

However, I think if we'd stayed I would have gained much
more. We own our own land, so I probably would have farmed,
been self-sufficient, and run my own business which is easier
there. If there were skills and resources missing, it could have
been brought to us. There is nothing to say we couldn't have
done it if we stayed. If you lose your history, you lose everything. If you always go away, you end up bringing up a lost
generation elsewhere. You have to bring it back to where you
started. I think our parents couldn't have brought it back quick
enough, and although a lot of people didn't mean to stay, we
now have an ageing population within this country and three
or four generations born here so - I guess it's home for the
majority.

To think positively about the future, I would say you can try
to make a contribution from wherever you are. You can make
a difference not just by staying in one place, but also, by
travelling elsewhere. When I went to the Gambia the children
could not get pencils and I was thinking I don't know anywhere
in the Caribbean where they can't afford a pencil - but it made
me want to do something. And it shows you that it only takes
all of us to do a little to help a lot. You don't have to feel like a
samaritan or a charity - I find that black people are the most
generous and unselfish race. Whenever I travel to black

countries, people always ask me into their houses and they don't know me. It's just a custom that they uphold in the villages. They are very kind to strangers. You can trust them and to me that is very rare - in England.

ANGELA GAY

Angela came to England in February 1966. She lived with
her grandmother in Barbados, and left to join her mother,
step-father and younger siblings in England.

In 1985 Angela went back to Barbados to settle. We
interviewed her on a trip back to London - about her
decision to return home and the experience of
readjusting to life there.

Going Back Home

Back Home

It was a dark, foggy February day in 1966 when my mother met me at the airport. Her first reaction to me was that I had gotten dark and I didn't look like the sweet little girl she had left behind. I had lived between my aunty and grandmother in Barbados. Life in Barbados was OK apart from a few unpleasant things that happened. The first thing I hated was that they pressed my hair. I used to have a bad reaction to this and got shivers up my spine and eventually they burnt me. I still have the scar on my face. I was also molested a few times by men - not sex - just fondling. I tried telling my grandmother but she did not understand and that made me feel horrible. Everyone thought I was lying.

London

When I first came to London, we lived in Ladbroke Grove in two rooms. One of those rooms was the kitchen. My mother took me into the big Victorian house and I thought, lovely, the whole house is ours. I rushed through the house and kept bumping into all these people and wondered what they were doing in our house. It eventually dawned on me that we only had the pokey room and the kitchen. When I came here my mother had two other children - my little sisters. One was two and the other one. They were very cute and friendly. The oldest of the two slept in the kitchen with me. In the middle of the night I would see these two eyes staring at me. They were rats. I couldn't sleep and neither could my sister. I kept her on the inside because she was younger. I started to have epileptic fits which I never had before. We later moved to a lovely three bedroom house in Southall. Southall is a predominantly Asian area, so we made new friends with Indian people and picked up their culture. I remember going to Saturday morning pictures to watch Indian films. My younger sisters even picked up some of the language.

Home Life

My mother had me back home and so I came into a situation where she was now married to a different man. She worked shifts and was always busy with my younger sisters - so it wasn't long before my step-father started to sexually abuse me. His abuse threw me out of the window. I couldn't concentrate because of what was happening at home and I became very disruptive. I didn't tell my mother because I knew I would get the same reaction as I did from my grandmother - so I kept it to myself.

My step-father started to give me money to keep quiet. I felt like a whore. I had to spend the money because I couldn't keep it or buy anything to take home as my mother would realise. I spent it all on chocolates and cream cakes and so I put on a lot of weight and got really fat. I eventually managed to stop it when I stabbed him one day with my school compass. After that he didn't try it again. My head became clear again and I could concentrate at school - however, things at home never really settled down. My mother was very strict and she always beat me a lot. I used to go to school with bruises and black eyes. It even got to the point where my mother accused me of sleeping with her husband, which made me glad that I hadn't told her what he had done to me, as I knew I would have got the blame.

Leaving Home

I came to England when I was eight and had to leave home by the time I was seventeen. Those years after leaving home were extremely difficult. I was homeless for a while. I can remember sleeping in toilets, on people's floors and in hostels. I went through a series of upheavals, trying to find money and accommodation. I got a job at Marks and Spencers. It paid £6.50, which was OK for those days. It paid for a room I rented in a house. But I found that I never had enough money, so I ended up stealing from the till. Of course I was caught red-handed and had mugshots, fingerprints, court case and probation - the whole lot. The judge told me if I had been a few months older I would have gone to jail. At the same time I was trying to study at college. I was doing my 'O' levels, but when I reached nineteen I left because I couldn't afford the fees.

Saving Grace

It was about this time that I discovered the women's movement. You could say that I was saved by the women's movement. It was my younger sister who introduced me to a group called Southall Black Sisters (SBS) and she was only fourteen at the time. She used to come around and I would plait her hair and we would chat. She told me about SBS. At first I was sceptical because I thought why are we organising as women when we have the whole of the black struggle to deal with. But my sister was so excited about this group and I was worried that they were filling her head with nonsense. Eventually, I got tired of her persecuting me, which she did religiously, and so I went to a meeting.

I fell in love on that first meeting. Not with anyone in particular, but I felt as if this was the best thing that had ever happened to me in my life. My life took off from there and I never looked back. I was quite naive growing up and things like sexuality, I just never thought about. I knew I didn't like men all that much because I had had few boyfriends. In fact, by the time I came across the women's movement, I'd already given up on men - but I just never knew that there was an alternative, that there were other people I could love besides men.

Could you tell me when you started the process of thinking that you might like to return to Barbados to live and what started that process?

Well, I got into this culture of drinking in my twenties. This was all part and parcel of being in the women's movement. I started drinking because I was depressed and drink was an escape from my problems. Also, I didn't like the way of life in England. I hated the racism and I hated not feeling like I belonged here. I never felt like I belonged. I didn't think about home that much, but I had been back a few times, but having become politically conscious and the fact that I liked women, I realised that it would be difficult for me to make a home in Barbados. I knew it would be damn near impossible to survive there - or so I thought. I was forever thinking where can I live, except England? I did not know of anywhere.

Over the years things gradually got worse for me. The women's movement overall started to collapse. The groups that I got involved in gradually began breaking up. People quarrelled a lot and I just felt like the place I'd found within these groups and the movement, was gone. I was totally disillusioned and I was feeling more and more that I could not stay in England any longer or I would drown. Also, my depression was getting deeper and my drinking becoming more serious.

The year before I left England, I had gone to Zimbabwe with a couple of friends. That was just after it had become Zimbabwe. It was an interesting experience, although quite rough, but it reminded me of home. The only difference was I did not speak the language - but everything else was similar. I thought to myself, if you are looking for somewhere to live, you might as well go back home because wherever you go, you are going to have problems. For the rest of the year, that was all I could think about. I decided to go home.

At first I was going for six months only to see how it worked out. When I bought my ticket and left, I think everyone was shocked but no one was more amazed than me. I sold my big boom box and bought a dual voltage radio. When I left, I took my clothes, my music and my books.

I thought I had enough money to last me six months but I ran out of money within two months. I had some savings still here in the bank which I sent for, but that also ran out - and the six months weren't even up yet.

By then I realised I had to find a job. I did find a job - easily, which surprised me. It paid well. It was a job in accounts, which I'd studied at college over here and it paid enough for me to get an apartment.

I found life in Barbados extremely difficult at first - because I was a 'woman's libber' I did not wear a bra. I did not press my hair. To the people out there I wore the weirdest clothes and they thought I was half mad. It took me a long time to start making real friends - I would say about five years - and even longer to make gay friends. I knew there were gay people in Barbados but meeting them was difficult. In fact it was a friend of mine from here who came over to visit who started the whole thing off. From London she had been put in touch with someone there and I met this woman who was really nice and after that I met many others.

By the time I got in touch with some gay people, I was

already in a relationship with a man. I never thought I would ever be in a relationship again with a man - but it worked out and we are still friends.

Barbados

The majority of people in Barbados are black (African), a smaller number Asians and about ten percent whites - who still rule. They are the richest and have the best. There isn't much mixing between the whites and the blacks unless you are a wealthy black. There is no segregation but the whites and the aspiring blacks, definitely keep themselves apart.

For years after Independence, the English ruled - but now it's very American influenced, though still very Bajan. There is a saying in Barbados that all a Bajan has to do is to read a letter from America and they develop a Yankee accent. They pick up anything American quick, and run with it.

Barbadians are very narrow-minded. If you come from across the waters - St.Lucia or Dominica - you are a foreigner, so I was most definitely not seen as a Bajan. I was a foreigner. They are also very intolerant of differences such as sexuality. There are gay people but they are not tolerated. I've been there fourteen years now and I find coming out a nonsense because everybody knows your business anyway. They figure things out very quickly, so you can't hide.

The lifestyle there is wonderful but a lot slower. Because it is a tourist-guided country, we are quite advanced in a lot of things. The infrastructure is quite advanced - even though there are still people without running water and electricity in their homes because they can't afford it. They don't have a social security system like England, so if you're not working, it's hard. When I first went there they had a system for those in work. If you should lose your job, you would claim six months unemployment benefit and you received sixty percent of your wages - which wasn't bad because you only get seventy percent of your salary after tax anyway. Anyhow, this system has now changed, and you only get three months unemployment benefit at sixty percent, the last three months you can only claim thirty percent of your salary. Beyond that, there are no other benefits. So everybody stays at home as long as possible. The majority of people live at home in extended families even after they are married. You just can't afford to move out into your own place.

I didn't have any problems getting work, but where I did find a problem was in my attitude towards work which is so different from the Islanders. Everything on the island is so slow, and everyone has this slow attitude, whereas my response was to get things done as quickly as possible. I can't spend hours on the phone talking when there is a pile of work on my desk. To them it might have seemed like I was trying to ingratiate myself. Now I work for private companies and they are driven by production, so you have to produce. This slow attitude is worse in government jobs.

The first job I had I got fired from because the boss was a player and I didn't like to play - so eventually he found a way to get rid of me. I have been promoted quite a lot in the job I am presently in - but not always with money. If my boss could get away without paying me, he would. Now I'm the boss and I basically demand my own wages. I'm still getting less than I want but I'm working on it.

Beach Life

Barbados has beautiful beaches but they are restricted. The beach property is very expensive, so the majority of people who have beach properties are white. They find ways of keeping the area private and keeping us out. They can do what they want because they drive the tourism industry. There

is even an advert on the television which tells you how to speak
to the tourist. They have cornered the tourism market and in
that sense they have pushed out the ordinary person who sells
a few corals on the street to make a living. They have these all
inclusive tours, so the moment the tourist steps off at the seaport
or airport, they are booked into coaches, hotels, sightseeing
tours - and are guided everywhere. So they could come to
Barbados and not touch a native. The ordinary people are
fighting for their little corner of the tourism market, but it's
easy to frighten tourists off - just mention harassment. I think
tourism is a bad thing for the Caribbean anyway and I have
always thought that even before I left England. The whites
have their little playground and we don't benefit at all.

Women and Progress

Women in Barbados are quite advanced in many areas. They
are accustomed to a lifestyle that women in England are
nowhere near. If you look at women politically in the western
sense, you might not think they are aware, but the Caribbean
has always been ahead when it comes to women's role in
society. The statistics say that fifty-one percent of households
are run by women - personally, I think it's more than that because
even when there is a man in the household, the women still do
the bread-winning and supporting. If you look within companies
- they might not be on the top rung - but they are everywhere
else on the ladder. If you stood at a roundabout and watched
the cars going by, they are mainly driven by women and they
are big cars too. The education system is in crisis because of
this. Throughout the Caribbean and perhaps in England too,
the girls are coming out better than the boys - in all subjects. It
used to be just the arts that girls excelled in - but now it's in
maths, science and business as well. In all walks of life you
will find that women out-number the men by three to one.

The talk now is that the men are in crisis and so too are the boys. They have tried to blame it on co-education. They say that boys are distracted by girls and that is why they are not achieving. I get furious. They pretend they can't figure it out. Sexism has a lot to do with it. Men do not know how to deal with the competition that they face from women. They don't like having to compete and they would rather opt out than compete. They feel totally threatened by women going forward and they are blaming their downfall on women rather than getting their act together.

I'm glad you mentioned that because the same thing is happening in England with the black community over there. It is exacerbated by racism - but I agree with you that the men have given up. But if they can't compete with their women, how are they going to compete with the rest of the world?

A lot of damage has been done to us in the past by white people and a lot of damage has been done to women by men - but the women have gotten themselves up, dusted themselves down and got on with it - whereas the men remain totally splattered. In the past they used to get married and tried to support their family - but now a lot of them are totally irresponsible and there is a lack of respect for women - to the point where a lot of women are now rejecting men and refusing to go on taking abuse. There are also some frightening things happening across the region of the Caribbean now where there has been a spate of violence against women in general - murders and rape. In some cases men have murdered their whole family and then committed suicide. Incest and child molestation has always been a problem and continues to be so. The pornography industry is growing and a lot of the young men are losing their heads on drugs which are now a growing problem. The stuff is pouring in from America, south and north. The police or coastguards can't stop it - usually they find a little bit, but that is just the tip of the iceberg.

Having said that, one of the things about Caribbean men which I must praise them for is that you do see them out with their children, or pushing a buggy - which is something you rarely see in England. They are quite willing to look after the children or do the cooking - so they are more advanced in that way.

So what advice would you give to anyone who is thinking of coming back to settle?

I would say give it a try. I would never come back to England to live. I have a lot of difficulties in Barbados, but they are nothing compared to England. The lifestyle here allows you to be more relaxed. One thing I've learnt since I've been here is to stop worrying about what everyone thinks. I think that was what made it for me - when I stopped worrying. At first I was making a lot of sacrifices to fit in. If I went to work and they commented on my dress, I would change it. Although I never got to the point of pressing my hair. When they commented on that, I just kept it short.

But, having said that, within the last few years in Barbados women have become so free with their hair. A few years ago all the women cut off their hair and looked good. The whole natural thing really took off. Some were even bold enough to go bald. Now they have started to grow their hair again, but still keeping it natural in plaits, twists or locks - anything except straightening. The majority of women here now are totally natural with themselves. They have gained a confidence that is so lovely, I just think - thank God I am in the right place. I love seeing natural people. It took me years to wear my shorts outside - but now I wear whatever I like. In fact, the women here, the bigger they are the more they show it off and you just look at them and say, "go girl."

Barbados is a small island and you might think it was limiting, but I don't find it limiting. There is so much going on. There are lots of festivals. There is always something to celebrate. You can get ragga music, dub, Calypso, and all the major artists from Jamaica come over here. If there is nothing to do, you can always throw a party.

I like going to the beach. I just call up a few friends, we all bring some food and drink and we just go lie on the beach and lyme. That's what Sundays are for and you go back to work on Monday feeling refreshed. You can go on moonlight picnics and if you ever come to Barbados, make sure you go for a cruise. The younger people might find there isn't enough noise and light for them - but for me it's perfect.

Every year somebody from England comes to visit me. I don't know anyone who has not enjoyed it. Some even come back again and again. I would never go back to England - except to visit.